History, People a
Eastern France

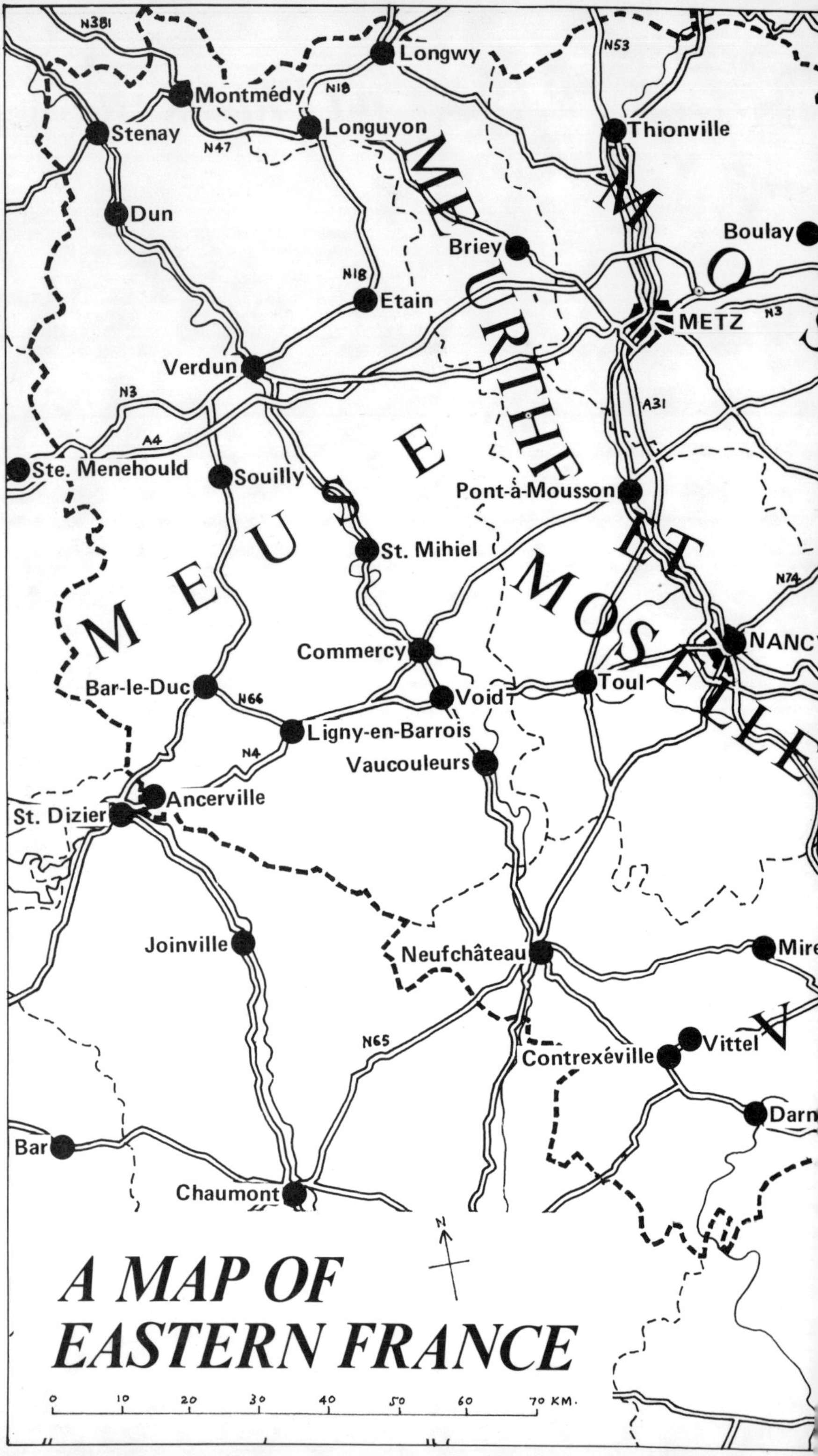
Longwy
N381
N53
Montmédy
N18
Stenay
Longuyon
Thionville
N47
MEURTHE
Dun
Briey
Boulay
MO
N18
Etain
METZ
N3
S
Verdun
N3
A31
A4
E
Ste. Menehould
Souilly
Pont-à-Mousson
MEUSE
St. Mihiel
ET
N74
MOSELLE
NANCY
Commercy
Bar-le-Duc
Toul
Void
N66
Ligny-en-Barrois
N4
Vaucouleurs
Ancerville
St. Dizier
Joinville
Neufchâteau
Mire
V
N65
Vittel
Contrexéville
Darn
Bar
Chaumont
N
A MAP OF
EASTERN FRANCE
0
10
20
30
40
50
60
70 KM.

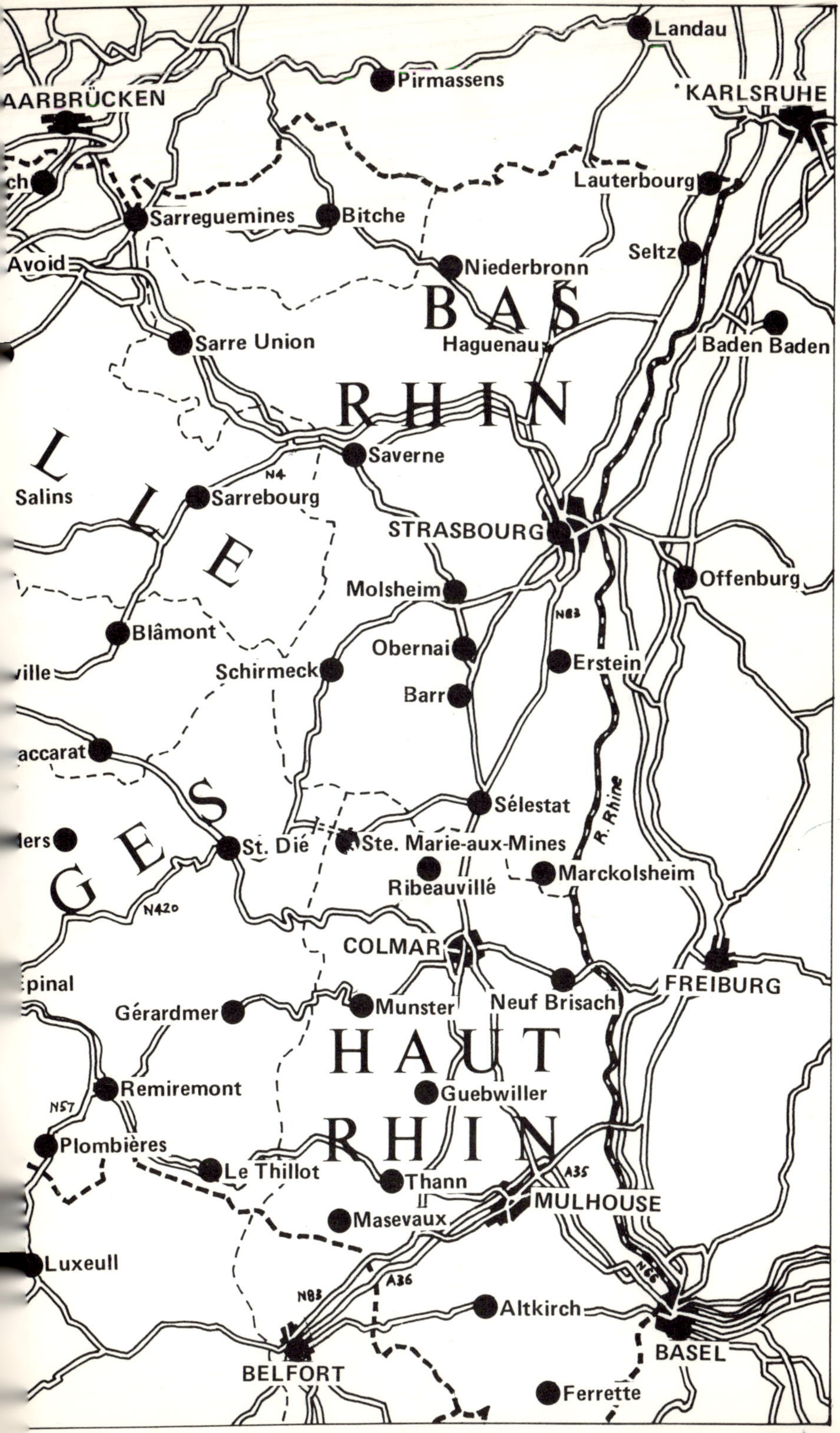
Landau
Pirmassens
AARBRÜCKEN
KARLSRUHE
ch
Lauterbourg
Sarreguemines
Bitche
Avoid
Seltz
Niederbronn
BAS
Haguenau
Baden Baden
Sarre Union
RHIN
Saverne
L
Salins
N4
Sarrebourg
STRASBOURG
L
E
Molsheim
Offenburg
N83
Blâmont
Obernai
Erstein
ville
Schirmeck
Barr
accarat
R. Rhine
Sélestat
S
lers
St. Dié
Ste. Marie-aux-Mines
E
G
Ribeauvillé
Marckolsheim
N420
COLMAR
Neuf Brisach
FREIBURG
pinal
Gérardmer
Munster
HAUT
Guebwiller
Remiremont
N57
RHIN
Plombières
Le Thillot
Thann
A35
MULHOUSE
Masevaux
Luxeull
N66
A36
N83
Altkirch
BASEL
BELFORT
Ferrette

Riquewihr – Fêtes des Vins

History, People and Places in

EASTERN FRANCE

Alsace, Lorraine and the Vosges

MICHAEL SHAW

SPURBOOKS LIMITED

Published by Spurbooks Limited
6 Parade Court
Bourne End Buckinghamshire

ISBN 0 904978 29 X

Designed and produced by
Mechanick Exercises, London

Typesetting by Inforum, Portsmouth

Printed in Great Britain by
The Garden City Press Limited
Letchworth, Hertfordshire SG6 1JS

Contents

Illustrations

Acknowledgements

This book was planned in collaboration with my old writing partner, Derek Pitt, who, alas, died before he could begin work on it. It was he who first interested me in Alsace and Lorraine. The book, as it appears, is my memorial to him, and I hope his pen's absence from its pages will not detract from their accuracy or appeal.

My thanks to my wife and to my stepson, Bruce Terry, for their company and help on several visits to the region to check details and to take photographs. And, as always, my gratitude to, and admiration for, the various officials of the *Syndicats d'Initiative* for their patient and knowledgeable quenching of my thirst for information. Finally, a word of thanks to the Photo Library of the French Government Tourist Office in London for help in filling one or two gaps in my collection of photographs of the two provinces.

1. The Place and the People

Alsace and Lorraine lie side by side, running north to south, with the tongue of the Vosges mountains making up the divide between them. The two provinces are so individual, both of them rugged in their own way, with their own dialects and customs built up by history and, not a little, by geography.

This is the eastern edge of France, where it bulges out like a piece of a giant jigsaw puzzle up to the banks of the Rhine, and it is less well known to English-speaking tourists than are the haunts that are blazoned in the pages of the tourist brochures. This is not surprising because Alsace and Lorraine are less obviously a 'tourist paradise', less geared to travel, less dynamic, less dramatic perhaps. It is even less easy to get there, for there are few direct flights and few direct trains. For many people this may well make it a more attractive area; where the big operators don't go becomes a place of greater peace and interest to the individualist, and there are many corners in these ancient regions that are sheer delight for the wanderer.

Alsace occupies the easternmost position down from the sharper slopes of the Vosges mountains across the fertile plain to the Rhine itself and the frontier with Germany. Lorraine spreads out more gently westwards from just below the Vosges peaks through a wide, mainly gently undulating, plateau to Bar-le-Duc and northwards to the Ardennes, Luxembourg and the dreadful industrial area of north-eastern France. Indeed, there are two Lorraines, the northern sector replete with coal and iron and covered with the sprawl of the resulting industries and the south, a great expanse of shining farmlands.

Both provinces spring logically and geologically from the Vosges. Many millions of years ago there was no Rhine, no Alsatian plain. A vast mountain range strode across the present gap between the Vosges and the Black Forest of Germany. Endless forests had grown there over the centuries, fallen, grown again, to deposit a thick layer of decomposing vegetation, later to be welded into coal. Then the sea had invaded, covered the original rock and vegetation, cast its own layers of sand and clay and chalk over everything for more millions of years.

In a new and violent convulsion of the earth, a mere fifty to sixty million years ago, the Alps came into being, savagely thrust out by immense forces, whose strength became dissipated with distance. The old mountain chain from the Vosges to the Black Forest was affected, and lifted more gradually to an estimated height of some 10,000 feet. The lower strata were pulled out of alignment, stretched, weakened and collapsed, forming a great rift that is now the plain of Alsace and the valley of the Rhine. The action of the sea, followed by rain, frost, glaciers, as the waters receded, formed the Vosges as they stand today, rounded, flattened, worn down to the age-old granites here and there, with the sandstones and hard packed gravels left behind elsewhere, with pockets hollowed out to form lakes like those called *Noir* and *Blanc* in the southern mountains, or with debris and moraine left behind to block valleys and create other lakes, such as that at Gérardmer.

Finally, and here time is measured rather in thousands than in millions of years, along with the cold periods that brought the glaciers, there came violent windstorms that carried in dust and sand and soil that settled as a deep loam (or *loess*) over much of the chalklands left behind by the sea. It is this *loess* that has formed the fertile agricultural lands of the plain of Alsace and the southern end of Lorraine.

For centuries the Vosges stood like a bastion between the two provinces, and only the northern col de Saverne provided a continuous usable route through the mountains. It was not until after 1918 that other rail links were established via the valley of the Bruche and through the tunnel cut at Sainte-Marie-aux-Mines.

This, in itself, meant that Alsace and Lorraine grew up with totally different identities and personalities. This difference was reinforced by history, though it has been history that has linked the two of them in people's minds.

* * *

Lorraine Landscape in Spring

The first historical link came after the great days of Charlemagne. Before that, Alsace had been only a Roman border province, a military area set there to face the savages, the Huns and the Goths. Lorraine, protected by military and mountains, had gained some Roman polish and civilisation. All this was destroyed by the invasion that followed the decline of Roman authority. In the course of time practical government came to be in the hands of the Frankish tribes. By 800 A.D. this was centred in the hands of Charlemagne, who built up a considerable empire. On the death of the Emperor's son, his realm was, by an inefficient Frankish custom, divided among his three grandsons. The middle section ran from the North Sea down to the foot of Italy. This was allocated to the eldest claimant, Lothaire, and so came to be called Lotharingia. Both Alsace and Lorraine, whose name is a corruption of Lotharingia, formed part of this hapless kingdom. Hardly had it been set up, by the Treaty of Verdun in 843 A.D. than Lothaire's two brothers started plotting to seize it. Alsace was soon snatched away and became part of the German sector of the old Empire. For seven

Typical Road in Lorraine

centuries it was cut off from France and never owed any sort of allegiance to that kingdom as it grew up.

In fact, Alsace developed a strongly independent civilisation and culture, based rather on the international character of the Rhine and its commerce than on any territorial loyalties. With the opening of the St. Gothard pass in 1230, the flow of traffic between north and south Europe tended to follow the Rhine itself, often, because of the difficulties of navigation on the upper river, along the trading road, that came to be known as the Bergstrasse, that ran along the eastern foothills of the Vosges. The line of old towns and cities, all filled with the evidence of luxurious merchants' houses, through Mulhouse, Ensisheim, Colmar, Sélestat and on to Wissembourg, shows the development and value of this route. Strasbourg, controlling one of the few ways across the wayward Rhine, grew up separately and stormily as a dominant crossroads for east-west as well as north-south trade. Its old name of *Strateburgum*, or "City of Roads", shows the basis of its importance, the source of its wealth but also the origin of many disasters, since it also became the main invasion route into France.

By the wealth they accumulated by trading and, doubtless, by lending money as well, the bigger towns of Alsace became powerful enough to shake off all feudal controls and to resist the efforts of Bishops, Barons and other rapacious bullies to lay hands on them. They established democratic institutions and the rule of elected aldermen. Art and letters were favoured and flourished until the bleak penumbra of religious controversy inflamed sensible men's passions in the late sixteenth century. Peace and prosperity then became precarious treasures. The peasants rose against the feudal lords and were ruthlessly and treacherously destroyed outside Saverne. The evils of ideology had, as usual, crushed happiness.

It was only in the north that Lorraine managed to achieve the prosperity found in Alsace. East-west trade had brought fortune to the towns that were lucky enough to dominate the roads, Toul, Metz and Verdun, and there it was the power of the Church that stood in the way of democratic development. These three cities are often called the "Three Bishoprics" because of the continuing authority of those spiritual lords, against which the increasingly wealthy burghers had to struggle before winning their right to self-determination about the end of the twelfth century.

The rest of Lorraine came under the domination of two powerful nobles, the Count of Bar and the Duke of Lorraine. The former was of ancient creation, the title dating from 954, and the latter was the self-made creation of an adventurer from over the mountains, one Gérard d'Alsace, in the 11th century. He established his headquarters at Nancy, and the family gradually came to rule almost the whole of Lorraine, absorbing the suzerainty of Bar in 1484. Only 9 years before that the Duke, René II, had defeated the King of France in a battle outside Nancy. His troops had borne as their standard the famous double cross of Lorraine, made even more famous centuries later following its adoption by General de Gaulle as the insignia of his Free French troops.

In 1552 the three Bishoprics felt themselves threatened by German princes supported by Charles V, King of Spain, Holy Roman Emperor and self-appointed Defender of the Catholic Faith. These three cities looked round for help, and Henri II of France, ever one to seize an opportunity for expansion, offered his protection. The French stepped in and quietly took over the government. Henri had to hold the cities against armies sent by Charles V, and then, having accomplished this, he stripped them of their local rights and customs, and made them part of France. "*Adieu Metz, Toul et Verdun!* " The appropriation was confirmed in 1559 and reaffirmed in 1648 by the Peace of Westphalia after the Thirty Years War.

During that War, Alsace, as part of the Germanic Rhineland, suffered considerably from the ravages of various armies seeking sustenance, as well as from the plague. Even Lorraine felt some effects of it when the Imperial forces invaded France in 1636, but that invasion lasted less than a year, and, by winter, the invaders had returned home. The Peace of Westphalia also brought to France some control over parts of Alsace, but the great city of Strasbourg still remained free.

The growing power of France under Louis XIV frightened the Emperor, and intermittent warfare continued between these rivals. In one campaign of this time, in 1674, the French general, Turenne, managed to trap the Imperial forces into a feeling of false security in Alsace. As winter drew on, the French forces, by a forced march of seventeen days through the Vosges, succeeded in falling, totally unexpectedly, on the enemy as he slowly withdrew to winter quarters across the frontier. This brilliant feat took place near Turckheim and the victory was a resounding, if not final, one.

* * *

From this time onward, peace, as well as prosperity, gradually returned to the troubled provinces. Even the Revolution had little effect here, though Metz was besieged, and taken, by Prussian forces. However, for our progress, history may now be left at this point until it again impinges fatally on the area at the end of the 19th century. Other events, having more local than regional importance, will be dealt with in later pages as and where their effects have more force, but the Franco-Prussian War of 1870 had dramatic and devastating results for Alsace and Lorraine, and so needs to be discussed here.

A little to the east of Verdun the road goes sharply down from the escarpment into the wide plain of the Woëvre, and thence, fairly flatly, to Metz. If you look back at the hills from that plain, you will find them, as the Germans must have done more than once in history, a daunting sight. It must have been an act of great courage (or fear of something worse perhaps) for the poor wretches who had to do it, to scale those heights, only to pour, probably, their good Teutonic blood on those inhospitable slopes.

The plain itself is littered with tiny German monuments from the campaign of 1870, some to individuals and others to regiments. A different, perhaps more gentlemanly war, this one, than that soon to come. The victors were different as well.

On the road to Metz is the insignificant village of Gravelotte – insignificant now, yes, but also important since it marks the end of the warfare of the past, and the beginning of the war of the future. There were two memorable events in the battle of Gravelotte. The first was that here came the last great cavalry charge of history, that of Von Bredow's Dragoons, all splendid in their scarlet and gallantry. Never again was a cavalry charge to be a gallant and romantic act. The second was that during the battle a truce was called so that the wounded could be collected and tended. Within a few days the sieges of the cities of Metz and Sedan brought into existence that form of warfare, so soon to be extended and developed, that required the long-range indiscriminate bombardment, of civilians within those cities.

The Franco-Prussian War is little remembered outside France. Yet its effect on the defeated French, and, especially, on the people of Alsace and Lorraine, was shattering. The cause of the war lay buried, probably, in the wily mind and the expansionist dream of Bismarck. The French Emperor, Napoleon III, suspected the German intentions and had tried, without avail, to persuade the French to rearm against this possible threat. The immediate fuse was lit when Napolean successfully thwarted Bismarck's plan to set Leopold of Hohenzollern on the throne of Spain. The "Iron Chancellor" of Prussia made public a telegram sent from Ems in which, by means of some re-wording, it appeared that the King of Prussia had insulted the French Ambassador. Napoleon reacted as Bismarck had foreseen; he declared war on Prussia and mobilised his forces as fast as possible.

This was not fast enough. The French plan – the eternal French plan, as will be seen later – was to advance in strength across the Rhine and strike deep into the heart of Germany. By the time they were ready to move they found the German forces already crossing the frontier to the north of Alsace and Lorraine. The concept of the later "*Blitzkrieg*" or "Lightning War" had been born.

The first encounter took place near Wissembourg on 4th August. The French 1st Corps withdrew towards the col de Saverne but were caught and defeated at Froeschwiller. On the same day (6th August) the French 2nd Corps was heavily defeated at Forbach. Their commander, Marshal Bazaine, with the remnants of his army, took refuge in Metz.

On 18th August the battle of Gravelotte took place. This was the last play of the French forces in the area, and the siege of Metz began. Marshal MacMahon, commanding the French forces in the north, attempted to relieve the city, accompanied by the Emperor himself, but lost his nerve when he learned of the size of the enemy forces, and withdrew to Sedan. There the French were surrounded by 1st September and surrendered the next day, Napoleon among them. This disaster destroyed resistance, although Metz held out, in spite of heavy bombardment, until 27th October. Paris fell on 28th January, 1871, and some French troops, still holding out in the Vosges managed to retreat to Switzerland.

Every fault in the French military machine was displayed in this brief war, its inability (or refusal) to face facts, its absurd self-confidence, its appalling slowness to move and to react, the fatal belief that French spirit (*élan*) must win the day. These faults were to reappear, and cost the country dear, twice more in the next seventy years.

By the terms imposed on the defeated France, almost the whole of Alsace and a good deal of Lorraine came under German rule, a state of affairs that was to last for some forty-eight years with effects that will be seen later. In the view of history, of course, this upheaval lasted only a short time and was one of a series of such events, but in terms of human feelings it must have been traumatic. In the literature of France at the time, in Maupassant's stories and in Zola, for instance, the Prussian is represented as a jack-booted bully, as an evil and sadistic enemy. How could the people of Lorraine and Alsace fail to be imbued with this idea? The power of propaganda is so strong that this, by itself may explain the lasting Frenchness of the Alsace, and the bitterness of the war so soon to be unleashed again on this corner of France.

2. Lorraine

If you drive south and east from Calais or Boulogne you have to pass through the dreary and traffic-filled roads of industrial northern France. By the time you reach, say, Stenay on the road to Verdun you are heartily sick of the scenery and the long, straight roads along which great lorries race dangerously. If you head even further east and come into Lorraine via Longwy and Thionville, the grey of mines and the grime of factories lasts even longer. It is not until you have penetrated much further that you come into the glorious and peaceful farmlands of the south.

The wealth, doubtless, comes from the north, along with the muck, but the beauty is in the rolling plain that spreads out from the banks of the younger Meuse and Moselle rivers. It seems no accident that Nancy should be the capital of this province; it has connections with both worlds, and it stands almost in the centre of it. It was chosen, it seems, by Gérard d'Alsace not because it was a strong defensive position, but because it was near the middle of his possessions. The first castle was built simply between two marshes to give it some protection. Perhaps this first Duke of Lorraine, like later French generals, was no believer in defence. The position in the world of modern Nancy is founded on industry even though its heart belongs to the eighteenth century.

All in all this is not a land of big towns and cities. They exist, of course, a few of them, and they have their own attractiveness and history, but surely the real Lorraine is found in the swelling curves of the countryside, the patches of woodland and the long sweeps of ploughland and grain, the broad valleys empty of noise save for the perennial conversation of birds, interspersed with the occasional warning shrill.

Spring is the time for Lorraine, just as the trees are being touched, little by little, by the sun, and their soft tones in varieties of brown and pink are being softened with a suspicion of green. Then the soil ranges in colour from terra cotta through burnt sienna to a rich plum, and the sprouting corn spreads a veil of green over vast rectangles. Fruit trees and blackthorn add contrast and highlight to the pattern, and the sharp outline of village spires and the geometry of red roofs add shape. This is a countryside for the water colour painter.

The lushness, however, is bred of rain. The fine days are glorious, but the really wet days are grim and endless. Let Maurice Barrès, that great Lorraine writer, whose name we shall meet again, describe them: '*Some days are withdrawn, monotonous, and then the orchards and the meadows and all the seed-lands, beneath a great sky laden with moisture, lie dreaming and turn to us a face of serenity, strength and sullenness. Springtime is sad in Lorraine, or at least austere; all the time the snow is still there in the sky and draws out its last farewells. Towards the end of the loveliest days, it is not infrequent for winter with a harsh sweep of wind to return and show his face among the clouds of the setting sun*'. So beware! But the beauty of the good days is exquisite when they come and makes up for all the cloud.

Then, when the sun is shining, keep away from the main roads. They are anyway crammed with those fast-moving, terrifying *camions* which make driving hideous. The side roads are a delight with constantly changing landscapes opening up round every corner. There are so many possible routes. Try, for instance, the road from Pont-à-Mousson across through Nomény, Lémoncourt, Vic-sur-Seille (an attractive old township) and the Regional Park to Mittersheim and Phalsbourg, where you can dine well at the *Erckmann-Chatrain* in the Place d'Armes. Look at the setting, very simple and unsophisticated, as you glide down to Aulnois with its handsome mansion, or, later, branch off to the Lake at Gondrexange; it won't be long before it is spoiled – there's a small camp site there already!

There is a whole network of little roads to the south-west of La Colline Inspirée, some 15 miles south of Nancy. These roads wind illogically through tiny villages and hamlets, between large acres of farmland, and lead you cunningly to that sudden semi-circle of

Aulnois-sur-Seille

wooded hills round Vaudémont and Sion that Barrès managed to establish as the spiritual heart of Lorraine.

It was not only Barrès: he was was only the most recent, and it was he who created, by his writings and speeches, the modern mysticism (or romanticism?) of the Hill of Inspiration. Before the Romans came, so it is said, the hill was a place of worship to savage gods, seized on, as usual, by the Christian Church when it arrived in the 4th century and adapted to the cult of the Virgin Mary, Notre Dame de Sion. During the 10th century, that age of supreme religious strength and conviction, while Vikings were thundering at the door, the first church was built at Sion, and the place became a centre of pilgrimage, or prayers for special occasions and events. By the 15th century, Sion's importance was so well established that it was in the name of Notre Dame de Sion, bearing her banner as well as the double barred cross, that Duke René II won his battle of Nancy against the French king.

* * *

La Colline Inspirée

War is part and parcel of the little church at Sion, not, in itself a building of much merit, but more a symbol in its own right of the independent character of Lorraine. It is here that the national fighting spirit of the region becomes visible in three separate, challenging statements carved in stone or concrete. The first, set in a black, wreath-like plaque, was erected in 1873, when part of Lorraine had been annexed by the Prussians, and, in local dialect, reads: '*It is not for ever*'. The second, above that one, set up in 1920, says: '*It was not for ever*', and the third, dating from 1946, has the words '*And now united for ever*'.

At the far end of the semicircle of hills is Vaudémont, its old castle a shabby ruin, where, on the old Telegraph Hill, is now a heavy, unambitious, unexciting monument to Maurice Barrès, with quotations from his writings round the side. The view is the notable part of the place; it embraces an enormous stretch of the countryside of Lorraine. '*As far as the eye can reach*,' says Barrès again, '*it sees only undulations: receding shapes that block the horizon; roads running and crossing as they lazily follow the valley-system of the land, fields incurved or arching like the stripes that the ploughs draw upon them*.'

It is not far away to the west that the warrior saint of France was reputedly born, at Domrémy, though surely not in the house that

Domrémy – Joan of Arc's Birthplace

now stands waiting for the *franc-payeur*. Joan of Arc was born in 1412, heard heavenly voices up in the Oak Wood where now stands a basilica with a rather fine, slender spire, went off to find the King (as yet uncrowned), win battles against the English, see her monarch crowned in Rheims cathedral, and then be captured by the Duke of Burgundy, by whom she was sold to the English. She then underwent the mockery of an ecclesiastical trial and the supreme penalty for losing a battle, death by burning at the stake, in Rouen.

Domrémy-la-Pucelle (Domrémy the Maiden) is an attractive little village set between wooded hills and the Meuse, and the assumed birthplace is an attractive little house, all set up with suitable 15th century furniture and notices that say that here the saint saw the light of day, and so on. The authenticity of it must, to say the least, remain in doubt. But '*si non è vero, è ben trovato*', as cynical Italians might say.

From this village, in 1428, inspired by heavenly voices, Joan plodded off northwards to Vaucouleurs, where the local military commander had his headquarters. After waiting some time (in fact, on and off for some months) she became impatient enough to set off, accompanied only by her uncle. But this was the country of the Duke of Burgundy, the King's chief rival, and she soon had to return. By now, however, her fame had spread wide about the district, and finally the Captain of Vaucouleurs Castle, Robert de Baudricourt, gave way and sent her to the King. Both Bernard Shaw and Anouilh have made good theatre out of the clash between Joan and Robert in their respective plays about the Saint, but their versions are, alas, almost certainly no more than that – good theatre.

Little enough now remains of the castle, some bits of walls and the crypt of the chapel up on the little hill. The Porte de France still stands, the gateway through which Joan set off for the Dauphin's court, or so they say, and death before she was twenty years old. However, were it not for the ghosts of that seminal encounter in 1428, it is doubtful if anyone except a devotee of ruins would bother to climb up the short, sharp slope.

The countryside is a joy, not unlike Dorset, rolling, rural, unspoiled. Most travellers are usually looking for more exciting, dramatic, unusual things, things to pander to his, or her, holiday uninhibitedness. Perhaps they press on southwards to Gérardmer a spanking place of entertainment with a lake to fill with sailing-boats

Vaucouleurs Castle

and water-skis, plenty of ground for camp sites, hotels and pensions, night clubs and discos; Gérardmer has its finger on current entertainment lures and includes excellent food at the hotel *Au Grand Cerf*. Perhaps they head for one of the old spas, such as Vittel, for instance, spas that are lagging a bit (no lake?) and so retain a little more of their old, plush, Imperial, swank even though the wealthy are now far less inclined to pay out good money to sip a glass of mineral water. The 'Michelin' always loves the old spas; they always get their three stars and it's a form of nostalgia that always appeals to the French.

The people of Lorraine are not ones for military adventure, not like the famous Gascons. Over the centuries wars have swept backwards and forwards over their land. There is no record of themselves initiating any war, especially those people of the ploughlands down in the south, any more than any other true farmer. The northerners of Metz or Verdun will fight perhaps, but then only to protect their possessions: they are the city-men, the wealthy, sweating after their *louis d'or*. In the past they fought for what was theirs. Now, more than any other Frenchman they dislike being regimented, called up and detailed by the State. The Cross of Lorraine is a romantic symbol still? Well, perhaps. But romantic symbols go with Lorraine and spring from the very soil – St. Joan, the "Good King René", the Polish King, Stanislas, who fell from Kingship and climbed back to a Dukedom by way of his daughter's Cinderella act, or even Maurice Barrès.

Behind this romantic image and the mask of simple rusticity, there beats a commercially aggressive heart and there works a crafty mind. Nancy, for instance, is for most travellers a most beautiful 18th century city, and Nancy is, for this reason, the acceptable capital city of this unworldly, agricultural region. Go there and you will find your 18th century elegance, for sure, but set as a smallish jewel in a pullulating ant-hill of an industrial complex, with all the accoutrements of that, civil engineering activities in abundance, new roads, housing developments, vast factories, and an undigested traffic problem. Yet the jewel in the centre is priceless, as is the classical food at *La Gastro Lâtre*, in the Rue Maréchaux.

Pont-à-Mousson greets the traveller with a modest and old-fashioned air. Here's the old Abbey, the ancient and departed University, the Place Duroc, quiet and peaceful. But just out of eye-range is an efficient, active and profitable industrial development, mostly quite new, but thrusting and ranging the whole world for markets.

Bar-le-Duc

This is clearly part of the style of Lorraine – the simple peasant girl who hears voices and goes off to conquer the world. That, at least, is the outward image. Certainly they are pleasant people to deal with and to talk to. More French than their neighbours of Alsace, more cordial, less hurried. Farmers, shopkeepers, tradesmen and artisans, just ordinary people with a touch of real kindness.

The past is the past, but its essence lives on. Feudal lords go into economic decline and family names wither away with the female line, but the spirit goes on, a ghost that can still dominate the modern, technological France of today, as it does in the United Kingdom. Look at Bar-le-Duc, once the home of the Dukes of Bar who were overtaken by changed habits and customs, as were the dinosaurs, who too failed to adapt as time moved on. The dukedom went in the fifteenth century, and yet . . .

And yet, up on the steep hill of the Old Town, though there is little enough left of the ancient headquarters of the Dukes apart from the names of the narrow streets, the Avenue du Château, Rue des Ducs de Bar, the place is still redolent of medieval life and attitudes. The ancient streets climb steeply up to a number of late

15th century houses and the old College of Gilles-de-Trèves. These buildings seem to underline, like a tombstone, the deadness of the Dukedom, since they date, as does the Eglise St-Pierre, from the last days of that age. The magnificent statue of a human skeleton by that fine 16th century local sculptor, Ligier Richier, presumably set up on the wall as a *memento mori*, is a sad symbol of the disappearance of the glory of Bar. Cobwebs, gilded cobwebs, like those in Miss Haversham's dining-room, almost seem to hang about the '*Ville Haute*'.

The modern aristocracy of Bar lives in modern palaces on the hill on the northern side of the Ornain. Here are the split level luxury homes of the wealthy industrialists, metallurgists and clock-makers, engineering component makers and textile men, the men who bring the new prosperity to the town. A parvenu aristocracy, no doubt, but they too have their dwellings high above the town, ignoring the visitor who stays, if wise, at the *Metz et Commerce*, on the Boulevard de La Rochelle.

In the centre, down round the river, live the ordinary folk, the workers, around the Place Exelmans. There and in the neighbouring streets on a Tuesday, you will find the weekly market. There are stalls offering every sort of goods for sale, even books, for this is a big market, where there are great crowds, and the traffic has to make way for it. The bustle and the liveliness make it a scene of tremendous vitality.

As well as a town like Bar, the countryside, surely, remains basically feudal – or is that incurable and blind romanticism, with the boys like wild things on their push-bikes and the young men roaring about on their Hondas? The villages are grouped about the old château, mansard-roofed in slate with little turrets at the corners, and, as has happened for century after century, human life is arranged by the tyranny of the seasons and, perhaps, the whim of the Big House. There are the herds of Friesians, those supreme milk-machines, munching the rich grass, accompanied, for butter-fat content, by a couple of Jerseys, the plough-harrow-sow-reap routine of the arable farmer. This must be the true Lorraine, this vast expanse of the agricultural plain that rolls southwards, mile after mile of it, down to the swelling hill-lands at the edge of the Vosges and the door-step of the Alps.

The truth, of course, is not quite so simple. The villages are seldom feudal in fact and the great house may well be a convalescent home. The villages are mostly democratically regimented, and crop rotation, dates of sowing and harvesting, the pecking order for machinery and labour, are arranged by majority vote. The smallholder must fit into the organisation or he will find himself bereft. But it works, this system, and seems to produce good profits. Collective handling brings results.

Only the large estate, the great landowner, whose stake often dates back through many centuries to some monastic right or to a royal (or revolutionary) gift, can afford to follow an individual line, and in an inflation-dominated age that is a situation that is beginning to fail, and building-sites are showing up just out of sight of the 18th century windows.

Historical greatness and grandeur are past. Verdun is over, though, in any case, that remains the glory of the whole of France and its Empire, rather than of this small and undemonstrative region of it. Yet Verdun somehow exemplifies Lorraine, the capacity to bear suffering, to go on, heads down, through the storm, through occupation, unreasonable demands, death. '*It is not for ever*,' that is the true motto of Lorraine, just as a two-fold cross marks its spirit.

3. Lorraine - The Northern Cities

The industrial north is hardly an area likely to appeal to the casual visitor; coal mines and iron works lack the appeal of the picturesque except, perhaps, to L.S. Lowry. In any case there is big trouble in the Lorraine smelting industry. The ore is difficult to extract and, in a time of recession, the mining is too expensive. Other sources, not far away, are more economic, and the Common Market trading arrangements have probably speeded the decline. Private firms are closing their furnaces. There is growing unemployment, especially in and around Thionville, in spite of Government efforts to attract other industries to the area.

In spite of this situation, it is the iron and coal that dominate the whole region to the north and east of Metz right up to the Luxembourg and the German borders, iron to the north and coal to the east. This ought to be an ideal combination, and for a century or so it has been. Pollution, clouds of stinking smoke, grim housing, all the concomitants of 19th century industry, have turned the romantic-sounding Moselle river into a nightmare as it drives up into Germany, though not thereafter. New industries have spread southwards from Metz, through Nancy and down to Epinal. These do not depend on the local minerals, but are chiefly concerned with cotton and other materials for textiles, and with electronics and light engineering.

For centuries during the Middle Ages Metz and Nancy were rivals for the supreme power in the area, and for quite different reasons;

Metz – Cathedral Square

while Metz was probably the most powerful commercial city of Lorraine, Nancy was the headquarters of the ruling Dukes. It was not until much later that it established its industrial claim.

Neolithic man was the first to settle in the area, after more primitive hunting tribes had passed through following the movements of their quarry. Then came the Celts from the Belgian region, soon to be followed by the Romans, bringing their peace and organisation. The tribe of Celts called the *Mediomatrices* by the conquerors had their centre, now named Divodurum, at the crossroads of the major trade routes from south to north (Lyons to Trier) and from east to west (Strasbourg to Rheims) which soon became Roman highways. While the Roman peace lasted so this town flourished. Later it came to be called Metz, by a contraction of the name of the Celtic tribe which had established it.

The great primitive townships all tended to grow round some point that dominated lines of communication. Not far away from Metz the tribe of *Trevises* had their strongpoint at what is now Toul, standing across the lower road from Rheims via the Vosges to the

Metz

Rhine, and further north, dominating the Meuse hills and the main crossing place of the river, was Verdun, the third of the powerful Bishoprics that exercised, for some centuries, a political as well as ecclesiastical control over the whole area.

After the Roman legions tramped away, the region was invaded by Germanic tribes, the Alamans and the Franks. Metz was besieged by Attila. These new conquerors occupied the northern half of the province, leaving place names in -ingen (or -ange) and in -weiler (or viller), while the southern half, still under Roman influence, has place names in -court, or -ville. Gradually, towards the end of the 8th century, the empire of Charlemagne enveloped the civilised world and brought peace for half a century, until shortly after the Treaty of Verdun, which though designed to resolve peacefully the rival claims of his grandsons to a share of the cake, brought only the inevitable family all-in wrestling that plunged Lorraine into war.

Because of its position, Metz managed to flourish, in spite of set-backs to trade and the destruction brought about by wars and rapine. In the 12th century it was strong enough to proclaim itself a free republic, with an elected President and government of aldermen, and so wealthy that it had to defend itself several times against its neighbours. Local aristocrats, amongst whom must, on occasion, be counted thc Bishops, as witness the depredations of His Grace of Strasbourg that will be recounted on a later page, often cast covetous eyes upon these moneyed burghers. If not covetous, the eyes were at least contemptuous and disdainful.

Typical is the story of the Duke of Bar who, supported by the young blades of his entourage, came riding into Metz after Mass one February Sunday and found the ladies of the city dancing in the jousting yard – a curious employment, one would think, for a winter's day! Yet Breughel's villagers often seem to have indulged in similar pastimes, even in mid-winter. Anyway, the gentry rounded up these ladies and stripped them of their clothes, leaving them, as Michelin delicately puts it, in a costume that is suitable neither to virtuous souls nor to the temperature of February. The menfolk of Metz, outraged as might have been expected, came out to defend the honour, as well as the health, of wives and daughters, fell on the jokers, chased them out of their city, and, not in a mood to appreciate the joke, drowned anyone they captured.

In 1552, along with Toul and Verdun, Metz became French, lost its freedom, resisted the siege of Charles V and settled down, in new colours to resume the prosperous trading operations it had enjoyed before this upset. Thereafter it underwent a siege about once a century, shrugged off their effects and went about its business.

Metz, today, is the financial capital of the industrial north. To look at its ancient centre, however, you would never believe this: it still looks and feels like a pre-war commercial capital, rather slow and cosy, still unmodernised, with narrow streets and small, provincial squares. Certainly the ubiquitous automobile has made its demands and has torn away part of the past for car-parks, but even these are small and yet seem to contain all the cars that present themselves. Outside the cathedral are bus-stops all mixed up with statucs. Shops are mostly small and unhurried, though a few big stores and Monoprix do make their appearance. Down by the Moselle are pleasant walks, and there is a fine esplanade with a terrace overlooking the river and Mont St. Quentin. Open spaces look out on to the older houses and churches, the whole picture somehow out of keeping with the bustling in-fighting that doubtless goes on behind the elderly façades. Given the old world disguise of Metz, it must be admitted that the place St-Louis, with its heavy arcades and tall buildings still does look its part as a centre of trade, even to the crowd of shiny parked cars. The town is blessed with a handful of good restaurants, notably *La Maison des Têtes*, in the Centre St-Jacques.

On the east of the city, the old Porte des Allemands recalls the medieval might of Metz. This gateway guards the entry to Metz over the river Seille and consists of two 13th century towers on the town side, topped by slate-covered witches' hats, of a bridge with a sharp-pointed arch, and of two later (15th century) and more massive, battlemented towers, on the far side of the river. An impressive, though much restored, group, displaying the military strength and pride that were once the boast of Metz.

The cathedral is fine, and should be seen, if only for the glorious collection of enormous stained-glass windows that range in date from brilliant medieval to striking modern. The building itself is a magnificent vehicle for these windows, being very tall, compact and unostentatious. Perhaps some good came from the Revolution's anti-clericalism, for great numbers of statues and other decorative fancies were destroyed at that time. So now it is just a big box made up of a kaleidoscope of colour as the sun pours through indigo and crimson on to the golden pillars and stone-slab floors. See how well the schematic glass-work of Jacques Villon of 1957 in the Saint-Sacrement chapel fits in with the simple medieval stories in pictures of the 13th and 14th centuries. The new main organ has only just been installed, a good example of modern builders' technique, but it is the lovely little 16th century choir organ that perches very high up, as though clinging there, in the south wall that will catch the visitor's eye.

Although, apart from a few medieval houses in the Place Sainte-Croix, there is nothing much to hold the visitor, except churches for the keen student, Metz remains an attractive city, simply because it shows so few signs of the current passion for concrete high-rise. Perhaps it is proud of its older look, or perhaps it shies away secretly from looking too far ahead, given its own past history and also the hard economic fact that the iron-ore is showing sharp signs of being too expensive to extract. Recession, maybe, is hiding round those windy corners of the city.

* * *

South of Metz, the Moselle river valley is still too industrialised to be the scenic pleasure it ought to be. Small factories, modern

Jesuit College at Pont-à-Mousson

housing, and somehow depressed farming areas line the road. Even the remains of a Roman aqueduct at Jouy-aux-Arches looks more like a bit of disused railway arch.

It is not until you reach Pont-à-Mousson that you feel stirred to stop. In spite of considerable damage done in September, 1944, there is an atmosphere of calm in the narrow streets of white-washed walls round what was an 18th century monastery. This was compelled to close its doors during the Revolution, became a Seminary during the last century, then a hospital, was almost destroyed by fire in 1944, and now, rebuilt, is a cultural centre where occasional displays are held. It is a rather grand collection of buildings in an austere Classical style, white with slate roofs, calm and self-possessed, which offers a particularly fine front to the wide river.

Nearby is the ancient University of Pont-à-Mousson. A University here? It may sound strange, a name never before heard of, but it is true. In 1572, Charles III, Duke of Lorraine, decided that a major effort was required to fight against the growing inroads being made in the Dukedom by the Protestant missionaries. So he founded this

University at Pont-à-Mousson to train clerics capable of withstanding the intellectual arguments of the brood of Luther and Calvin. It was only a small unit and was housed in the buildings there beside the bridge whose Cour d'Honneur, almost totally rebuilt since the War, is a pleasant quadrangle like that of one of the smaller Cambridge Colleges, Peterhouse, for example. The University lasted only a little more than a century. The Thirty Years War brought plague to the town, and the students packed their bags and decamped, and, in 1699, this '*Grove of Academe*' was transferred to Nancy.

Across the bridge you soon come to the Place Duroc, which, while in name reminiscent of a dingy station on the Paris Métro, is a singularly attractive memorial to the same Marshal of Napoleon's army, a native of this little town. This square, or perhaps circus would be a more accurate word, since it is a large circle in shape, is surrounded by 16th and 17th century houses, of several storeys, set above a squat arcading that shelters shops and cafés. Only the great Town Hall, very impressive for so small a place, is of the 18th century. The other houses are much in keeping with each other, and form a fine coherent whole. One should look especially at the House of the Seven Deadly Sins, with large figures of these vices, and at the late Renaissance Town House of the Dukes of Lorraine, called romantically or suggestively, the *Château d'Amour*. The broad central area of the Place is planted with shaped evergreens and beds of flowers.

Early in September, 1944, part of General Patton's Forces were poised to cross the Moselle here. They were confronted by a German armoured division which, having cut the bridge, took up a strong position on the Butte de Mousson, a tor some four miles to the east of the river. In the flat local countryside this hill has a commanding position. For about a fortnight the two forces pounded at each other, as well as the unfortunate town that, to its sorrow, had a large foot on each bank of the river. Meanwhile the worthy general doubtless addressed some fairly unprintable adjurations to his commander in the field. At last the Americans managed to cross the river higher up and, outflanking the Germans, forced them to retire from the Butte, and so set the Allied drive eastwards in motion again. The strategic value of the Butte de Mousson had, in the Middle Ages made it the site for one of the castles of the Dukes of Bar. The ruins are still there, in spite of the devastations of more recent wars and of more modern weapons.

It is difficult to get away from war in this part of Lorraine. Verdun

Pont-à-Mousson – Place Duroc

Toul Cathedral

is not far off, but that deserves a separate chapter. However, from Pont-à-Mousson the road almost due east takes you over some delightful hilly country into an area also bitterly disputed in the '14-'18 war, round St-Mihiel in the Meuse valley. Today the route takes you through the peace of the most spectacular of the Regional Parklands of Lorraine, with, in the hills above the Moselle, the sharp little valleys and bluffs of what is, with somewhat unreasonable vanity, called "*La Petite Suisse Lorraine*". Then, up near the Lake of Madine is found the sharp hill of the Butte de Montsec which is surmounted by an impressive American monument to those forces that, in September, 1918, managed to iron out the German-held salient of St-Mihiel which, throughout the War had been a menace to the French, especially during the siege of Verdun, since it had blocked the main road along the Meuse to that city.

St-Mihiel has a vast Abbey church and some imposing Abbey buildings. These almost all date from the 17th century, when they were rebuilt with financial help from Louis XIV himself. Since this was the birth-place of Ligier Richier, Lorraine's finest sculptor, it is natural that one of his great religious groups, '*The Virgin Mary held by St John*', dated about 1530, should be in the church.

Toul suffered both at the beginning and in the later stages of the last War. Perhaps it suffers more now from the stream of heavy traffic that goes constantly, east to west, along its southern fringe.

It owes its importance to a curious geological event. Some two million or so years ago, the river Moselle flowed westwards past the hillock on which stands this city, and it ran into the Meuse. Then, for some reason, some stirring of the earth, the river changed its course and carved itself a new valley to the east, down to the rather lower valley of the Meurthe river, which it dominated and whose channel it took over. The old valley running westwards and the new valley running east created an easy route for travellers and trade, and so Toul flourished.

As at Metz, the wealthy burghers, about the 12th century, became powerful enough to oust the government of the Bishop, and to set up their own republic. Thus did the second of the three Bishoprics liberate itself from its ecclesiastical master. Toul, however, never quite achieved the same degree of sheer power as did Metz, and it had already begun negotiations with France before 1552, when Henri II moved in to the three Bishoprics, invited certainly, but a guest like a mouse in a piece of cheese, and absorbed them. Until recently, Toul has maintained a quiet, unremarkable course, mainly as a market town for a large region. Now industry is moving in, on a grand scale, out of the greater complex of the Nancy area. Among others, the Kléber-Colombes group has recently established a giant new plant there, thus bringing much needed new jobs.

In the centre, though, Toul still seems slow and countrified, without too much bustle, its road signs directed, it seems, more towards misleading than to assisting the unwary motorist. It has a magnificent Gothic Cathedral, greatly but splendidly restored since the War, very bright, with almost no stained glass inside, and with a breathtaking west front which is, alas, so crowded about with buildings that it is difficult to see it well. It is a small scale Rheims or Rouen, intricate weaving of stone into glorious shapes. Next to it is the 18th century Bishop's Palace, now the Town Hall, which ought to be a noble building but which looks tired and liable to collapse. The *Syndicat d'Initiative*, beside the Cathedral, is seldom open, and really the whole place seems little interested in wooing the tourist trade. Yet it is a strangely pleasant place.

4. Verdun

Because of the Wagnerian grandeur of the holocaust that it witnessed in 1916, and because it is a testimony to the resilience and courage of man, as well as to the sacrifice of human life, Verdun deserves a separate chapter.

The Romans established a fortress, *Virodunum Cadrum* there, and it was prosperous enough, as Roman power declined, for Attila to sack it. To the Treaty of 843, dividing Charlemagne's empire between his three grandsons, one part of which was Germania, may perhaps be attributed the almost mystical importance that the place has had for German invaders.

It stands on a bluff overlooking the Meuse and dominating the crossing place. The hills along the west bank of the river and the heights not far away to the east that provide a natural bastion above the Woëvre plain have made it a stronghold that has often been harried by invaders throughout history. It was besieged during the Thirty Years War and was afterwards fortified by Vauban as the keystone of the eastern defence line that this great military architect created for Louis XIV. During the Revolution it was besieged by the Prussian Army and only fell when its commander, Beaurepaire, died, either committing suicide in despair or being murdered by the suffering townsfolk. Then, in 1870, under siege again, Verdun held out longer than the other strongholds of the east, for two months against the Prussians. It was, perhaps, a fortunate miscalculation of the Germans that they did not annex this fortress along with much

Verdun

of the rest of Lorraine, since it enabled the French to turn it into the powerful defensive position it became, at least in its basic structures, by 1914, and so to create the rock on which the German offensive of 1916 foundered. Some historians believe Verdun to have been the real turning-point of the whole War.

The old town is perched up steepish streets on its little pinnacle of hill. There you find the Cathedral, a rather uninteresting building, refashioned and mauled about in the 18th century, though its Romanesque crypt, brought to light as a result of German bombardments, has some fine capitals and a well-preserved doorway. The Bishop's Palace, used as offices and a library, is an austere and, now, somewhat seedy 18th century building whose courtyard must once have been a splendid sight when the Bishop himself was a true Prince of the Church and the courtyard filled with the carriages and servants of visiting dignitaries. It was in this Cour d'Honneur that the first German shell of the 1916 siege fell, damaging the corner of the Cathedral.

Not far away is the vast Vauban Citadel which shows his style of fortification to perfection, the great stone *glacis* reinforcing the

Verdun – Monument of Victory

hillside and the sharp-pointed key angles to the forward positions, all mathematical, precise, and in the best tradition of French logic. Prior to 1914 an enormous subterranean stronghold was fashioned within Vauban's walls, and this served, throughout the siege, as the command centre for all the French defences, safe enough from bombardment, though not from the disastrous news that poured in during the first weeks of the fighting. Those troops and the wounded who did manage to find their way back from the battle zones used it as a rest centre. It is possible to visit this underground headquarters.

The lower town, sprawling along the banks of the Meuse, is a pleasant, lively, small country town, not presumptuous or demanding in any way, but somehow easy-going and welcoming. There is a wide quay on the west side that leads up to the old Porte Chaussée, one of the medieval town gates, that still stands sentinel at the bridge after some six hundred years, with its big, crenellated towers, not as grim as the Porte des Allemands at Metz, but tough and rugged, as it has needed to be, still there after war upon war. Standing against the hillside, at the back of the Porte, is the imposing Monument of Victory, at the top of seventy-three wide steps. The great stone figure of a medieval knight leaning on his sword is mounted on a broad stone tower that contains the Golden Book of the names of the soldiers who fought in that defence. On the other side of the river is a small square, the Place Chevert, by the riverside and, a little beyond, the Town Hall that contains a War Museum.

Out in the hills to the north-west and north of the city lie the tortured lands of the vicious fighting of spring and summer of 1916, in which the French armies managed to hold back the ferocious onslaughts of the Germans in their attempt to roll up the whole Western Front from this southern outpost. This is still a horrifying landscape where trees, mostly pines, have been set to hide the pitted hillsides that are still incapable of sustaining more useful plant life. Contemporary photographs show this landscape with nothing whatsoever standing, as a featureless and pock-marked void. The wonder of it is that men did live and fight in the horrors of this ghastly world.

Hundreds of thousands of men, French and German, fell on these hillsides. The memory of the French is preserved, as are the shattered remnants of those not otherwise identified, in the Ossuary of Douaumont, whose great central tower, some 150 feet high, stands out like a white finger pointing to heaven. Not far away is the Fort of Douaumont, one of the two main front-line fortresses built on the very edge of the sharp declivity up which the invaders had to fight

Verdun Battlefields – Fort de Vaux

their way. This fortress and that of Vaux, some 3 miles distant along the ridge, still give a terrible picture of the conditions undergone by the besieged.

These forts had been designed to withstand any sort of major attack, equipped, as they were, with artillery and machine-guns that could enfilade and cover every corner of the defensive walls. However, during the preceding summer, the French High Command had become infected with an antipathy to defensive warfare, a recrudescence of a prevailing pre-war romantic worship of constant aggression. The result was that the defences of Verdun were deprived of their defensive weapons, which were sent to the northern front. The enemy, on the other hand, was building up enormously strong artillery with which to blast the defenders out of their forts. Indeed, when their attack began in the early hours of 21st February, 1916, they put down a barrage such as had never been seen before and will not be seen again.

* * *

On 25th February the Fort of Douaumont fell. Although orders had been given from the Headquarters of Marshal Joffre himself that the Forts of Verdun were to be put as speedily as possible at full strength, these orders had never reached the local command. A small detachment of Germans climbed up to the outer defences of the fortress and were astonished to find no defenders. The only French troops in the fort were artillerymen serving the few guns still there. The fall of Douaumont sent waves of shock through the whole of France. One result was the urgent dispatch of General Pétain to take command of the battle. This was the same man, the 'Hero of Verdun', who became the symbol of French defeat in 1940.

The German attacks continued, though greatly abated by the exceptional spring rains which reduced the Plain to a morass and made the movement of their heavy guns a nightmare. This situation gave Pétain a chance to establish his lines of communication with his sources of supply. The only road into Verdun out of range of enemy guns was that one from Bar-le-Duc which was never designed for this sort of traffic. Pétain put every able-bodied man to work, and by skilful traffic control and continuous repair of the track managed to move guns, ammunition and reinforcements up to the front line. Later this road became known as the *Voie Sacrée* (the Holy Way), and today, as it runs peacefully up to Verdun, every kilometre stone is set in a carefully tended verge and is surmounted by a casting of a French soldier's helmet bound with laurel as a memorial, created in 1921, to the heroic defence. The main memorial on the *Voie Sacrée*, a somewhat lacklustre stone stele, stands by the roadside at Le Moulin Brûlé.

Early in that dreadful April the main German attack was diverted along a new line of approach, on the western bank of the Meuse river. Here the French defences were centred on a low hill called, for some ironical reason hidden in the mists of the past, le *Mort Homme* (the Dead Man), and another rise (Hill 304), not far away, which held the available French artillery. On 14th March, six German divisions made a full frontal attack on this position, after a saturation bombardment that ought to have killed every living creature.

What is so terrible about World War I is that such tremendous heroism and wastage of life took place to possess or defend half an acre or so of barren hillside. The *Mort Homme* is a case in point. On a notice up there by the topmost monument mention is made of the trees that have been planted there because, owing to the devastation of the battles, '*toute culture étant impossible*' nothing else could be grown. It is said that in these hills round Verdun was the highest density of dead per square yard ever known, before or since. The *Mort Homme*, a rather pleasant and solitary place now, together with the area round Vaux Fort, must have supplied some of the more ghastly of these statistics.

At the end of May, *le Mort Homme* finally fell, too late to enable the German drive on that front to gather strength before the whole siege petered out. There was, however, a final and furious German assault on Vaux. This went in during the first week of June. The outside defences of the fortress were over-run on the 3rd, owing again to lack of artillery and shortage even of machine-guns. Then came the most horrifying part of the whole campaign, a desperate defence, mostly in darkness and underground, against flame-throwers and toxic smoke, in the corridors and casemates of the fortress.

On the 7th only 250 defenders were still left alive, and their surrender was accepted with military courtesy. Five months later the fort was recaptured. The remains of the fort today are filled with the memories of those terrible days as you penetrate into the subterranean regions. Perhaps the most pathetic memorial there is a plaque erected to the last pigeon to be sent off, on 4th June, by Major Raynal, commander of the garrison. It carried a message that read: '*We are still holding out but are undergoing a terrible attack with gas and smoke. It is vital we are relieved. Arrange visual communication with Souville which does not respond to our appeals. This is my last pigeon.*' The pigeon got through to Verdun and, dramatically, died immediately after delivering the message. A relief column was indeed sent out but was virtually destroyed by the enemy in that ghastly lunar landscape of shell-holes. Even now, among the pine trees, the ancient holes and trenches can be detected. It is still a grim and frightening place.

After capturing Vaux the German forces pressed on to what might have been the decisive conquest, that of the inner line of forts on the very edge of the hills leading down to Verdun itself. The first of these was Souville, a small strong-point that was, however, the command post. It was in this attack that the gas *Phosgene* was first used. Fortunately the defending troops had recently been issued with a new gas-mask that could withstand this new weapon, and the attack was thwarted. Then the start of the first Battle of the Somme on 1st July made the German High Command withdraw strength from the Verdun front, and gradually the pressure eased. The mystique of Verdun is still enormous and the whole area, constantly visited, is carefully, almost religiously preserved, not always successfully, let it be said, though this is perhaps not the fault of the French.

One place that ought to be as moving as anywhere in this great expanse is the so-called *Tranchée des Baïonnettes*, the 'Trench of Bayonets'. After a night of violent bombardment the French company defending the Ravine de la Dame seemed to have totally disappeared. It was not until after the end of the War that their trench was discovered, entirely filled in. In a line were seen the points of bayonets, spaced regularly and showing just above the earth. Below were found the corpses of the missing company, dead at their posts and buried, it is supposed, by the German bombardment. An American benefactor has raised, above the trench, a heavy concrete structure that is quite out of keeping with the place and has somehow quite destroyed the atmosphere.

These hillsides are a shrine to French valour, to the spirit of endurance that is the mark of the men who went through so much hell. '*Ils ne passeront pas*', 'They shall not pass' was the slogan that caught the public feeling of the time and expressed the will of the Army, at least in hindsight. And with pride the monument on Le Mort Homme is engraved: '*Ils n'ont pas passé*' 'They have not passed'. Verdun is a symbol of man's unconquerable spirit and, as such, must make an appeal to all nations.

5. *Nancy and the South*

Until the comparatively recent industrial growth of the area, Nancy had developed almost by chance. In the 11th century it became the stronghold of the Duchy of Lorraine simply because it was somewhere near the centre of the scattered possessions acquired by Gérard d'Alsace. It was there, in the marshy lands that gave him the river as a moat, that he built a castle and, perhaps as a safeguard for his avaricious soul founded several monasteries. Destroyed by fire in 1228, the castle was rebuilt, and, by the 14th century the town that had grown up clinging to the skirts of the stronghold, had been surrounded by a powerful bastion. Of this the Porte de la Craffe still stands, a massive and sombre building in which can be seen those relics of man's inhumanity of man, torture instruments, dungeons on whose walls desperate men have scratched their claims to sanity and humanity. It is a terrible place on which succeeding ages have grafted their insignia, including of course the famous Cross of Lorraine.

Over the centuries man has poured out his violence and blood over these few acres of ground. All that time Nancy has, almost by its own efforts, remained the capital of the Duchy of Lorraine, and later of the province, through thick and thin, through war and the later onslaughts of industrial might at the hands of Metz. In the 18th century the ruling Duke, Francis III was bought out by Louis XV of France for what seems now little more a 'mess of pottage', an offer of the duchy of Tuscany. Then Louis conferred the Dukedom on

Nancy

Stanislas Leszczynski, his father-in-law and the deposed King of Poland.

It is to Stanislas that Nancy owes that artistic attraction, its marvellous 18th century architectural heart. It's all so unexpected; you go down a dull, heavy, 19th century street, redolent of the comfort of good eating and wealth, and suddenly you are, without time to take it in, hurtled into the delicacy and style of the Age of Reason. The matter-of-fact grey stone, a bit tarnished and blackened now, of the self-satisfied Empire gives way to Palladian grace and spaciousness, to ornate iron-work and to long vistas and elegant facades. There is no interval, no preparation for the violence of the visual and cultural switch. Even the side of the Arc de Triomphe, erected by Stanislas as a token of gratitude to Louis, looks dirty, slatternly and dull at first sight. It needs just a few steps to see how splendidly it fits in to the total concept. And it is all glorious, all of it, the Arc itself, but, especially, the two squares which it divides and links.

The story of Stanislas and his daughter, Marie, is not far from the

Nancy – Fountain and Wrought Iron Screen

classic fairy tale. He was elected King of Poland while still a young man but was later turned out in a pacific political upheaval. With his daughter he settled in Wissembourg, and they lived there in straightened circumstances until 1725, when a messenger came, to announce that Louis had selected Marie to be his wife. Apparently the choice was not, in fact, the King's but that of his Chief Minister, the Duke of Bourbon, and his mistress, who hoped that their selection would become their catspaw and ensure their continuing dominance of the State. Poor Stanislas was hard put to it to send his daughter off properly equipped to become the First Lady of France. By dint of heavy borrowing he managed it, and she was married in Strasbourg Cathedral with all due ceremony, but by proxy; Louis, who was only 15, remained in Paris.

Stanislas, himself, did not suffer from the situation. He may have lost a daughter, but he gained a Dukedom, or, in truth, two – those of Bar and of Lorraine. And he was provided with an ample financial allowance to maintain his new estate. Much of this money went on the beautification of his capital, Nancy.

He had already something to build on; successive Dukes of Lorraine had added buildings, the fine Ducal Palace, originally of the 13th century but since destroyed, and rebuilt by René II at the end of the 15th, mostly destroyed again in the Revolution but lovingly reconstructed in 1850. Its magnificent ornate gateway, flamboyant and yet carefully planned, is the finest feature, but the carving in galleries and balconies is also splendid. Next door is the Church of the Cordeliers, which contains the tombs of the Dukes of Lorraine, some of them magnificent examples of the sculptor's art.

Then, towards the end of the 16th century, there was a lot of building done, a whole 'new' town raised beside the old fortified city. This all suffered considerably during the Thirty Years War. After 1648 the damage was laboriously repaired and, not content with simple patching up, Duke Leopold started the proud range of buildings that line each side of the Place Carrière, the ancient jousting place of the Dukes and in neighbouring streets. These, however, were modified later when the whole area was rebuilt.

Stanislas set himself, with the help of his architect, Héré, his ironsmith, Lamour, and his sculptor, Guibal, to create from this basis a sumptuous centre for his capital. A new square, in the noblest and most splendid of Baroque styles, was established to the south of the Place Carrière, to which it is linked by an Arc de Triomphe in the accepted Roman mould. This square is now called the Place Stanislas, although until the Revolution, it was the Place

Royale. It is dominated by the great bulk of the Hôtel de Ville, built in a sober Classical style, ordered, rather solemn, and this is matched by another impressive building at the far end of the Place Carrière, the Palais de Gouvernement, in which the Governors of Lorraine lived once.

The Place Stanislas is completed by large blocks of buildings down each side and up to the Arc. The austerity of the architecture is relieved in part by the variations of the lines of window openings on each level, by the balustraded tops of the buildings themselves, and by the ornamental swatches of foliage on top. But what really gives the basic uniformity its delightful contrast is the wrought iron work, the beautiful screens and lamps and coats of arms, and, at each corner, the florid rococo fountains set into, and surrounded by, the ornate black and gilded flamboyance of the arches and gateways. The three craftsmen have here contrasted with, and complemented, each other so as to create a satisfying group, something you will, probably, see nowhere else in the world.

The Arc de Triumphe, Stanislas' tribute to his father-in-law, somehow fits in to the total conception, even though the style is quite different. The side facing the Place Stanislas has an imperial Roman appearance, with heroic figures on the top. The other side, though still ornately carved, has a simpler top, in the form of a

Place Stanislas – Nancy

Nancy – Arc de Triomphe

balustrade whose pillars are in the strange shape of great chain-links, a curious composition.

The Place Carrière is long and formal, plane trees forming an avenue in front of the standardised but not stereotyped 18th century terraced town houses on each side. In the distance stands the Palais de Gouvernement. Spreading out from its huge Classical facade with its plain pillars and studied sobriety, there is, at the level of the terrace that runs the length of that facade a fine curved colonnade whose two arms link the main building to those at the side. This colonnade, set on sober Ionic pillars, carries a flat roof, balustraded and decorated with big flower vases and figures out of Classical mythology. It all forms an impressive and perfect statement of the control and logic of the age.

Round this central part of the city there is a lot to look at and relish, much good eighteenth-century work, graceful and severe, scattered here and there, long-lasting buildings as well as beautifully designed, the sort of building that some modern architects, doubt-

Nancy – Place de la Carrière

less, will dismiss as 'trite' or 'old hat', as 'decorative' but hardly '*machines à habiter*', although I have a feeling that Le Corbusier would certainly have approved. As a minor achievement, look at the Place d'Alliance with its large, serene town houses of the wealthy. Magnificent stuff, and work of real quality.

In Nancy, too, the museum enthusiasts and painting buffs will find much to tempt them – a very fine museum of Lorraine's history, archaeology, medieval relics, ironwork, and some splendid etchings of Jacques Callot, in a good art gallery with some satisfying modern works as well as primitives.

There is not much else to hold the visitor. Modern Nancy is a bustling, busy place. There are some decent hotels, the most modern being the *Frantel*, a high-rise, high-price palace by the station. Around it, as is usual round stations, there are several small, unpretentious, even seedy, hostelries waiting, in all probability, to be pulled down to make way for more Frantels, but suitable for the impecunious. Just outside the town, near the race-court, on the Neufchâteau road, is an excellent municipal camp site, called '*de Brabois*', beautifully set in a woodland and with good modern accoutrements. But it's under attack; housing developments look as though they are all set to urbanise it – the mechanical diggers are at the door!

Probably Nancy does not set out to be a tourist trap; it is such a thriving industrial centre that its time and energies are better spent on speedier money-making pursuits. Since 1870, when it was left unabsorbed by the Germans, it has been expanding ever outwards, swallowing up old domains like Laxou, Villers and Vandoeuvre, which now are just housing estates, and this growth, like the lunatic development of cancerous cells, goes on still. Vast housing estates are still sprouting everywhere, and enormous new roads are being laid down. This part of the city is depressing, and perhaps one appreciates the peace and sense of style of the centre the more because of it.

Within reach of Nancy is a clutch of rather magnificent country mansions, called châteaux, homes as opposed to the *châteaux-forts* which had military might and strategic significance. If you go out on the N57 road towards Epinal, and if you can disentangle yourself from the autoroute that goes off to Lunéville, you can turn left at Baraques to Fléville. Here is a neat, Renaissance house, built on the site, and incorporating the square keep, of a 12th century fortress. Here, too, and especially inside, can be seen, if not the hand, at least the mind, of Stanislas, in the décor, and more especially in the chapel. Warning: it is open to the public only at weekends and on public holidays.

Further away, Lunéville has a sumptuous, early 18th century, palace, built by the architect Boffrand, one of Mansant's pupils, and Mansart was the creator of most of the vast reconstruction that is present day Versailles. No need to say more! The château of Lunéville, designed for Duke Leopold of Lorraine, and later a favourite haunt of Stanislas, has something of the nobility and pompousness of Versailles, long sandstone wings springing forward from a central, typically Mansart, block, that contains, as does the Louvre in Paris, porticoes and arcades leading to the gardens beyond. The central building has a classical pediment and four Ionic pilasters, and the long arms of buildings, gradually stepping lower as they come further away, make a magnificent Cour d'Honneur which contains the mounted statue of one of Napoleon's generals, de Lasalle. It was at Lunéville that Stanislas died in 1766, the signal for Lorraine to revert to France.

Another castle is Haroué, to the west of the Epinal road, and on the way to the Colline Inspirée. It is much advertised and therefore not difficult to find. It is another of Boffrand's designs, again with slated roofs. This is not a little Versailles, however, and the way it is set in square, ornamental water-channels, rather than in defensive moats, makes it look like a refugee from the Loire Valley. But it is an impressive building and a pleasure to see, though the interior is mainly for devotees of the 18th century.

All the way up the Moselle valley as far as Epinal, along the N57, which carries a lot of heavy traffic, can be seen the signs of fairly recent industrialisation. This, added to the destruction of two wars, has turned the area into a rash of new building, much of it dismal. The township of Charmes is an example. After the dreadful destruction of the last War, the town centre was lovingly rebuilt, but it is a rather sad relic set within an encirclement of housing estates. There is little enough to indicate the tremendously valuable roles played here in two wars.

In August, 1914, the lessons of 1870 had still not been learned, and the French High Command had grandiose plans for the liberation of the occupied parts of Alsace and Lorraine. Inspired by the belief that French *élan* would inevitably, and miraculously, bring victory, a swift advance was launched which, almost unbelievably, entered Mulhouse, only to be ejected quite quickly, by violent German counter-attacks. Simultaneously the French First and Second Armies pressed on swiftly from the defensive line of the Meurthe as far as Sarrebourg and beyond. There the Germans had prepared a strong defensive line, against which the tide of French progress was murderously shattered. Withdrawal to the Meurthe line was the only alternative.

This line had been fixed and constructed after the débâcle of 1870. It consisted of a line of strong-points along the hills as far as Epinal, and then again from Toul northwards to Verdun. In the middle, with Charmes as the centre, a gap had been deliberately left in the hope that any attack from the east would be attracted there and funnelled into a sort of massive ambush to the west. Hindsight makes it seem such an obvious trap that no intelligent enemy could possibly fall for it.

In fact, and unbelievably, the Germans did drive forward into the very jaws of that gap of Charmes. There, in the face of strong attacks by the 1st and 2nd Armies, which seem to have been made too early (that accursed *élan* again?) to seal the mouth of the trap, the German advance hesitated and petered out. After the Battle of the Marne in September, the war in this region became fairly static all along the line until the dark days of Verdun in 1916.

Just outside Charmes is a hill called the Signal de Charmes. On it is the Monument de Lorraine, behind which is a '*Table d'Orientation*' which gives a full picture of the Battle of the Gap of August-September, 1914. The view is fine. Charmes itself suffered again in 1944 when the German forces, in full retreat, set fire to the place in what appears to have been solely an act of spite.

The valley of the Moselle does not become really attractive before Epinal because of the low key industrialisation that has taken place. As for Epinal itself, it is probably unfair to criticise, because war, here too, has ravaged it, especially the last war when it was fought over in June, 1940, bombed by the Allies in 1944, and deliberately destroyed by the enemy before they withdrew. The fact is, however, that it really is dull, in spite of its long history of industrial success and its constant expansion. It began its industries as the centre of picture reproduction printing, to which has more recently been added cotton processing and wire-drawing. There has been a lot of activity and wealth here, still is indeed, though perhaps soon the crunch may come with the regression that is hitting France as well as much of the rest of Western Europe.

Epinal is well placed on the two sides of the Moselle, and it stands there below the wooded slopes that enclose the valley. The ancient castle, now only a few stones, occupied a spur that creeps right into the town, and its grounds are a '*pleasaunce*' for the people of the place, who dine contentedly at *Les Ducs de Lorraine*, on the Quai St-Sérot. Another fine open space is Le Cours, down by the riverside, beautifully kept and adorned with some splendid, sometimes rare, trees. Of old buildings, understandably enough, there are few, though the Place des Vosges, with its arcaded buildings and that 16th century mansion, from whose balcony the old justiciars watched the public hangings, is attractive.

The Basilica of St. Maurice, damaged, rebuilt, added to, remodelled, expanded and subjected to the indignities of 19th century refurbishing after the destructiveness of the Revolution, shows little of the glory it once had. For a long time after its foundation in the 11th century (only one tower remains from that period, and that has been capped by a 19th century steeple), it was part of the Community of the Ladies of Epinal, an aristocratic foundation for the noblesse of Lorraine. This, at first, was the centre and mainspring of the town. It was a place of retreat for world-weary (and perhaps crusade-weary) wives and daughters of the great families, not a nunnery, more of a temporary bolt-hole. The church hasn't very much to interest the visitor except the cavern of a Gothic porch which seems to recede like an underground tunnel on the north side. It is called the Townsfolk's Porch (*Portail des Bourgeois*).

Somewhat less than 20 miles upstream from Epinal stands the town of Remiremont, at the junction of the Moselle and the Moselotte. Another textile centre with small factories, Remiremont has still some attractive old streets, the rue Charles-de-Gaulle, for instance, arcaded and flower-decked in summer. Here, too, was a medieval retreat for gentlewomen, this time an Abbey, whose Abbess was a Princess of the Holy Roman Empire. None of the other residents, it seems, took any vows, and they led a life of comfort, and even pleasure.

From Remiremont the countryside becomes more hilly, more exciting, and your choice of places to see is limited only by your interest. South-west leads to the spa country, with several old watering-places in easy reach, if they interest you as much as they do Michelin. Probably the most satisfying visually and historically is Luxeuil-les-Bains. There was, for instance, in the 6th century a tough Irish saint who founded a monastery there with a fierce discipline for his followers. He was forced to leave the country for telling the Duke of Burgundy what he thought of his morals. There

Outskirts of Gérardmer – Vosges

Gérardmer Lake

are some rather fine 15th century houses here, and it is worth a visit. Which is more, I think, than can be said of Plombières.

Most visitors will probably make their way up into the Vosges to Gérardmer, though the wise, and those with the time, will press on up the Moselle valley as it heads for the round and shaven head of the Ballon d'Alsace, the third great mountain of the southern Vosges. This part of the river valley, up to Le Thillot, for example, from which you can double back to Gérardmer, is the most beautiful area and one not to miss if possible.

But Gérardmer is where most tourists are going. It is certainly the best centre for southern Lorraine and for the highest regions of the mountains. On the face of it, it has everything – a superb position, grand countryside, the largest lake in the whole region, masses of hotels and camp sites, winter sports facilities, as well as every requirement for summer entertainment. What it lacks is character, personality. Perhaps it is too anxious to please. It is totally committed to the tourist trade, and places that pander wholeheartedly to the tourist trade can hardly expect to escape the eternal insignia of prostitution.

At least, with Gérardmer, this is forgivable. In an excess of unbelievable bestiality, the Germans in retreat tried to destroy the place entirely. Some 600 of the populace had been deported in the autumn of 1944, and the rest had been herded into a single block in the centre of the town. The rest was systematically burned. Almost nothing was left standing. The French troops entered the town on 19th November, 1944, and found it still smoking.

But then, such is the resilience of men, especially where their livelihood is concerned, that the place was quickly rebuilt. Fortunately the Germans were unable to destroy the lake and the great circle of pine-covered slopes surrounding it. This was the townsfolk's livelihood, their slice of the cake. That and the textile trade, mainly in household linens, tablecloths and napkins, which was quickly reconstituted, modernised with Government help, and is now the money-spinner that comes second only to tourism in terms of trade.

In the great Ice Ages, glaciers formed in the heights above Gérardmer, and, later, as they melted they scored out the clear-cut valleys. One, in particular, sliding down, inches at a time and over centuries, hollowed out lake beds and deposited silt and rocks to block rivers and streams. Thus were created, down this valley that springs from the very neck of the Hohneck, which is the second largest of the Vosges, the lakes named Retournemer, Longemer, and Gérardmer. At the same time the river Valogne became blocked and was forced to break out into another valley. That splendid cascade known as the Saut des Cuves, leaping in flood from giant wash-bowl to wash-bowl, was the way the river found to empty itself down into its new valley. It can be a very fine sight.

This is all a magnificent landscape with every sort of exciting viewpoint, plenty of walks and drives, right up to the top of the Vosges (something of which will be described later, when we consider the eastern side of the mountains). It is no wonder Gérardmer is so popular, and no wonder it is so full in the summer (and winter!) season. Hotels there are in abundance, at all prices, and camp sites, too. If the latter are all full, don't be persuaded, except in dire need, to go to Fraize, which is a dim little town anyway, and the camp site is scruffy. The one at Corcieux may be better, but it is mainly for permanent stayers, and struck us as somehow sinister.

6. Alsace - Saverne and the Northern Vosges

In the very north of the Vosges, Lorraine sneaks a curious slice of territory along the German frontier, which makes it permissible, perhaps, to cross the border into Alsace in this chapter and to glance at the northern hills before considering the whole of the province. The northern route is the one that centuries of travellers have used to pierce the barrier of mountains; the Col of Saverne provides the gentlest of the passes leading from the north part of France to the great trading point and Rhine crossing-place that is Strasbourg. The first railway link ran that way and the Marne-Rhine canal claws its way over the pass there as well.

Although the Moselle valley north and south of Metz is an industrial horror, so polluted between Metz and the Luxembourg and German borders that it is almost a discomfort to breathe, the vast, undulating plain to the east of that city is immediately fresh, rustic and clean. There is not much of note there, but the contrast with the Metz area makes it all the more delightful. Farmlands share the countryside with big forests, often State forests now, cultivated for timber but available meanwhile for long, and often solitary, drives and picnics. Over towards Sarrebourg there is a line of large lakes running north and south, from that of Mittersheim, a very large expanse of water almost completely surrounded by caravans and tents, down to Gondrexange, where the holiday gearing is in its early stages.

Sarrebourg was a Roman military station and staging-post. Today

Phalsbourg

it is a pleasant enough, but totally undistinguished, little town. Phalsbourg is more interesting. Because of its position on the edge of the mountains and at an important cross-roads, it was fortified by Vauban. Two town gates remain as reminders of this. Another memorial of its military past is the enormous square in the centre. This is the Place d'Armes, presumably the parade-ground of the garrison. Its size suggests that the garrison at one time must have been a large one. This great square, not even filled now by motor-cars at the height of the tourist season, is appealing and a little pathetic as it looks nostalgically at past glories.

From there the road climbs over the pine-covered slopes of the mountains and into Alsace, running down easily into Saverne.

Such an obvious route through the barrier of the Vosges, between the main bloc of the mountains to the south and the more northerly, and lower, range, must offer commercial advantages in any age, and the Romans were never slow to appreciate the value of trade. The merchant followed swiftly on the heels of the legionary as he has in the growth of every empire, not least the British. So it was that a

Saverne – the Rohan Palace

trading-post, named *Tres Tabernae*, was established where the hills met the broad Rhineland plain. This caravanserai became fortified and, through the centuries, became stronger still, watched over by its castle, its name corrupted into Saverne.

A castle was built on the pinnacle overlooking the town certainly by the 11th century, probably before. It is such a dominant place that it is hard not to believe it must for ever have been fortified in some way. The present ruins are the relic of a later reconstruction. They provide a sight of one of the better preserved mountain-top fortresses in the area and are well worth a visit. The views are magnificent, as they should be after some of the stairways that have to be climbed!

The remodelling of the castle was the work of a particularly worldly Bishop of Strasbourg named Manderscheidt. From the 13th century up to the Revolution, Saverne was the property of the immensely powerful See of Strasbourg, whose Bishops were Princes of the Holy Roman Empire. Their summer palace was here, and it was one of them, the Cardinal Louis de Rohan who, in 1744, rebuilt the earlier palace as the lavish building that now dominates the town. This is the centre-piece and most striking feature of Saverne, and, perhaps, of northern Alsace. It is, in some ways, even more impressive than the other de Rohan palace in Strasbourg.

Austere formality and overwhelming size are the keynotes of this Neo-Classic structure. This is best seen from the cramped garden at what might seem to be the back. There the facade is much as it was originally designed and built. There the inevitability of the sequence of windows and pilasters would be irritating were it not for the ornate central portico with soaring Corinthian pillars. As it is there is a grandiose harmony about the whole design, as mathematical and imposing as one of the great preludes and fugues of Bach. The other side, the one that faces the old market square, called Place de Gaulle, was somewhat remodelled in 1852, when the building was designated a sort of grace and favour residence for widows of high state employees. Now the main part seems largely unused, only the two wings in use to house a museum, the Youth Hostel, and various administrative offices of the Town Hall. It is a sad and lifeless building, a hollow shell of grandeur. The late 15th century Tower of Cagliostro, with the Chapelle St-Michel, which stand next door and almost look down on the parvenu château of the Rohans, form a much more sympathetic unit.

Saverne – Market Day

The best restaurant, serving Alsatian specialities is the *Jean*, in the Rue de la Gare, while the main street is hilly, bright, not too modernised, and leads inevitably to the focus point of the market square and the château. The market is a real local function, jolly, active, with local horticulturalists selling produce and the usual gathering of the professionals. There are a few good houses, notably the Katz house in the main street. It is perhaps a little self-conscious and dolled up, and it shelters the *Syndicat d'Initiative*. Gardeners will be interested to learn that Saverne is a centre of the rose-growing industry, and there is a very fine rose-garden on permanent display in the town, as well as a botanical garden up on the Col.

Saverne is still a commercial centre for the area, as it always has been through all the vicissitudes of history, fought over, wrecked, occupied, liberated, and then occupied again. One of the most poignant moments of its long history must have been in 1525. Then the desperation action of the peasants to shake off their feudal ties and to win a fair deal from their lords, a revolt called the rising of the '*Rustauds*', or peasants, came to a bitter end here. The poor wretches were besieged by the Duke of Lorraine in Saverne and at the end of their tether they accepted a guarantee by the Duke that their lives would be spared if they yielded. As they left the town, disarmed, they were attacked and slaughtered by the Duke's forces, and the countryside ran red with their blood and stank with their rotting corpses. And this, it is said, in spite of every effort by the Duke to control his men.

Withal that Saverne wears a cheerful face. Perhaps this is a philosophical approach to possible conquest. Perhaps it is an appreciation of the value of goodwill. It makes it a pleasant place to visit, and from which to tour the northern hills. In the *Hôtel de la Marne* we have found one of the more attractive resting-places. It overlooks the Canal de la Marne au Rhin along which enormous barges sail sleepily past through locks which just contain them and where everything seems to proceed so slowly.

* * *

The northern Vosges lack the drama, if that is the right word for any part of these mountains, or at any rate the height, of the main mass further south. And the towns, by and large, lack the more obvious appeal of, say, Kaysersberg or Riquewihr, but they thereby enjoy the benefit of attracting, to our enjoyment, fewer tourists.

La Petite-Pierre

You will see very few of the mammoth Germany luxury coaches, filled with *lederhosen* and Tyrolean hats, too often the uniform of the "*reise-prizers*". In spring the traffic has hardly started, and this is the best time to come.

Both Neuwiller-lès-Saverne and Bouxwiller, to the north of Saverne and just below the escarpment of the mountains, have their attractions, the former mainly in the Romanesque remnants of the Abbey church of St-Pierre-et-Paul, and the latter in its handsome old black-and-white houses. Round here, however, the typical Alsatian buildings are being too obviously done up, presumably to lure the visitors. Perhaps this is most evident in Ernolsheim, where every house seems to be done in brilliant white with jet black beams. One even doubts the authenticity of the latter, a doubt increased by the mock-1900 street-lamps.

From Neuwiller an attractive little road (D.134) climbs gallantly up through vast forests that open up here and there to give sweeping views of the clefts of valleys sliding down to the plain, and leads to La Petite-Pierre.

In spite of its curious name, this was a well-found medieval stronghold that made full use of the unusual geological structure of the hills here. Spurs of the mountains stand out like peninsulas, with narrow ledges that lead to a rounded knoll. So here there is a small town perched on one outcrop, and it is dominated by its castle standing on a separate and higher spur, the whole being carved out by ancient glaciers into a natural motte and bailey castle. Little enough of the fortress itself now stands, not enough indeed to allow one to work out its lay-out. It covers a large area, big enough to have provided the ultimate refuge for the whole population and their stock. Water was stored in an underground cistern under the rock of the castle. Surely it can have been captured only because of treachery or starvation, for it seems such an impregnable site. The little old town is peacefully attractive, and outside the walls, along the line of the D.7 road, a number of holiday homes are springing up. Before long the lake of Imsthal, beautifully situated among great trees down in the valley below, must be swallowed up in developments, or be turned into a vacation centre.

Northwards from here the landscape spreads out in huge sweeps of woodland, mainly of beeches and pines, leading in time to part of the wide glass-making stretch, gravelly and sandy, of the Vosges. On the way, on the D.12 leading to Bitche (and who can resist the temptation to go there?), you pass the 'Twelve Apostles' stone. This is an ancient 'standing' stone, as they are called in Western Scotland, the object of some distant, uncharted religious cult. This particular stone was carved in the 18th century, as the result of a vow, with the figures of the Apostles, surmounted by a cross. Soon after this, still going north, you travel back into Lorraine. One of the old provincial division posts can be seen by the road a little further on.

Bitche, when you get there, is a dull township, better known to the French Army for the vast training area near-by than to the tourist. It was fortified in the 17th century by the indefatigable Vauban as one of his line of protective strong-points. It may have proved effective then, but hardly counted when the real crunch came in 1870. The citadel still sits there overlooking the town, but it looks as though it never saw a shot fired except in practice.

Here we are almost on the frontier with Germany, and the world shows every mark of its violent past. Ruined castles dot the hills and form the links of a chain of eyries belonging to every kind of bird of prey. It must have been a savage and cruel world, and one is bewildered by the sheer effort involved in the building of so many

The Apostles Stone

Bitche

fierce fortresses on the sheerest and highest pinnacles. You have only to climb up to Falkenstein or Fleckenstein to marvel at human resourcefulness and resilience. These two strongholds, though they lack the ease of approach of Haut-Barr at Saverne to which you can drive, have much more atmosphere, haunting echoes of grim deeds and violent men.

Falkenstein owes more, perhaps, to nature than to man, both in the building and the destruction. The sandstone outcrop that sticks out, as a result of some massive, primeval, geological folding, at the top of this natural tumulus, was hollowed out here and there by water to form caverns and niches that were incorporated into the fabric of the castle. Now all you need are strong legs and will and a head for heights to visit what remains of this 12th century creation, struck by lightning and set on fire in 1564, with further destruction done by French troops in 1677. It is a long climb to the Guard Room, a water-carved cave with seats roughed out round the walls. Then you climb up stone stairways and along the knife-edge that the ruins now form high above the surrounding hills. There are vast views, of course, even stretching, so they say, as far as Strasbourg cathedral on a clear day.

Carving by French Prisoners at Falkenstein Castle

The buildings, or what remain of them, were used as a prison for recalcitrant Frenchmen by the Germans at various times after the invasion of 1870. Beautifully carved names and inscriptions bear witness to these captivities. Altogether this is a most impressive place that leads the imagination into the wild fastnesses of the later, and probably even darker, Dark Ages.

Not far away the more massive Fleckenstein beckons the strong-limbed up another mountainside. It is more complete than Falkenstein, with rooms carved out of the sandstone still in reasonable repair. There is even a small museum. But somehow it lacks the strangeness of Falkenstein. At any rate it doesn't lead you in the same way on a narrow pathway high, high above the sheer drop of a thousand feet or so.

* * *

Up here in these vast forests there are two vacation centres, entirely different the one from the other but both offering good holiday scope. The first is the Étang of Hanau, a superbly beautiful lake set among hills of pine trees that march in ranks down to the

Étang de Hanau

water's edge. This is developing fast into a boating, fishing and camping paradise, but is difficult to penetrate. The other is the small spa town of Niederbronn, originally founded by the Romans and brought back to use in the 16th century. It is similar to countless other small watering-places that came to their culminating prominence in the wealthy over-indulgence of the late nineteenth century. Spa waters are not everyone's cup of tea, but Niederbronn offers the tourist a number of good hotels and a wonderful position not far from fine walking areas and the highest peak of the northern Vosges, the Wintersberg.

From the neighbourhood of Fleckenstein the D.3 climbs up again to the Col du Pigeonnier, through woods and valleys and villages that live by forestry, saw-milling, and, frequently, fish-farming. The Col is the last pinnacle before the lowlands, and from it you peer down on to the great plain of the Rhine lands.

Tucked away in the furthest north-eastern corner of Alsace there is one lovely old town that must be visited, Wissembourg. As much German, perhaps, as French, it has managed, by some means, to

Wissembourg – Place du Marche aux Choux

Wissembourg

Wissembourg – Old Quarter

exist in what must have been, over the centuries, a hell's kitchen of war, bestiality and betrayal. Perhaps the citizens learned to use a craft greater than that of their neighbours. In any case, it stands there, much of it unchanged since the 16th century, as a fine example of Alsatian building styles, a place to linger in and wander in. Along the edge of the little river, the Lauter, is a line of attractive houses, mostly in traditional mould of beam-work and plaster with tall, tall roofs with little dormers let in, but there are even some in more modern Mansart-style French architecture, dating, doubtless, from after the union of Alsace and France in the latter part of the 17th century. The scrap of garden by the river adds to the beauty of the scene. This riverside walk leads on to the oldest part of the town, the Bruch quarter, where the water is lined with some magnificent and very tall merchants' houses, very picturesque, so picturesque, indeed, that it was used as the setting for a film, "*l'Ami Fritz*".

Back towards the town centre is found the Hospital, in part of whose buildings the ex-King of Poland, Stanislas Leszczynski was living in 1725 with his daughter, Marie, when the unbelievable happened to bring them both from the near poverty in which they were plunged; the Duke of Antin came as messenger from Paris to say that King Louis XV had fixed on Marie for his wife. The story has already been told, in the chapter on Nancy, of the Cinderella who became Queen and of her father who was made a Duke. Marie played her part in providing an heir to the throne, and Stanislas provided Nancy with its splendid city centre.

As for Wissembourg, there are other good groups of houses. The main street, modernised a little, is still fine though swamped with traffic, and the old ramparts offer a satisfying tree-lined walk. Apart from Wissembourg, there is not much, on the plain, to hold the visitor in this north-eastern corner. And so, back to Saverne, dinner and bed.

7. *Alsace*

That great mountain range that, millions of years ago, joined the Vosges to the Black Mountains, cracked, split and collapsed in the middle to form the plain of Alsace and to offer a wide valley for the Rhine. It is therefore the Rhine that dominates. The remaining mountains race down, sheer, to meet the river, down in a headlong, helter-skelter dash, until at the lower levels they smooth their lines and ease their slopes to allow the great vineyards to cover them. Along the heights the pinnacles of shattered castles still keep watch, pitiful Cyclops, one-eyed and spent, unless they have been expensively restored into a sort of Disneyland for the benefit of the "*reisebüro*" proprietors from over the Rhine. Down on the plain they share their task, equally pitifully, with remnants of the ill-fated Maginot line, soon, we have seen, to be auctioned off – for what purpose, dear bureaucrats? Who can possibly want an underground casemate today? To grow mushrooms, perhaps? Surely not for the mysterious processing of white cabbage into *choucroute*, so beloved of the locals.

There is so much history, so much legend and folk-myth about this land, its roots so deeply buried, the home of Neolithic man, a Roman outpost, a medieval mass of small possessions, of robbers turned custodians and crooks fashioned into aristocrats. These castles perched crazily on pinnacles of mountains bred strong-armed bandits, fighters, thugs, highwaymen battening on the rich trade that clung to the north-south highways of the flat-lands and the

Pfister House in Colmar

east-west arteries curving along the valleys through the hills. Pocket handkerchief dukedoms grew up, independent, pig-headed, tough, and it was not until 1648 that they were coalesced into some semblance of a province of France, after the Thirty Years War, by the Treaty of Westphalia. Then it was not until 33 years later that old, proud Strasbourg bowed its head to Louis XIV and Vauban raised his line of fortified towns along the line of the Rhine – Fort-Louis, Strasbourg, Neuf-Brisach, Huningue.

Alsace remained physically separated from France, at least at its northern end by the still legally independent dukedom of Lorraine. This gave it a certain arrogance and self-determination vis-à-vis the central authority. That individualism still exists. Someone has said that everyone in Alsace goes by the name of Schmidt, but drives a Peugeot. Certainly the natives speak French and German, as well as their own localised German dialect, with equal facility. It is normal to go into a shop and ask for, say, a baguette of bread in academic French and be given the price as "*eins fünf*". And, of course, German tourists swarm here.

Given this history, it is surprising that the people should have any deep feeling at all for France. And yet they do. During the long years of German occupation, from 1870 to 1918, for instance,

Decorated Roof in Colmar

Colmar, where as much or more German is to be heard than French, bred a number of stalwart characters who, in the face of Prussian punishment, upheld and preached French culture and customs. It may have been because the invaders tried too hard to recreate what they believed to be a basic Germanness in the country. Perhaps it was more the traditional independence, or even pig-headedness, that provoked this militant opposition, the spirit of the 16th century '*Rustauds*', who dared to challenge the might of their feudal lords.

Several French authors have found the Prussian victory of 1870 a traumatic experience. It may have been the unexpectedness of the attack to those self-satisfied and prosperous bourgeois of Paris, more likely the disastrous showing of the French troops and the dreadful surrender of Napoleon III with his Army at Sedan. The extent of the psychological wound can be gauged from the way these writers probe it again and again.

Alphonse Daudet is typical. His "*Contes du Lundi*" contain a number of tales about this event. The first one, 'The Last Class' sets the tone. Here a lad arrives late for school one morning and finds the teacher in his best clothes and all the village elders sitting at the back of the class. The boy learns that this is the last class of French that will be taught, since the Prussian authorities have ordered that only German shall be taught in future.

The story ends: '*Suddenly the church clock struck midday, then the Angelus. At the same moment the trumpets of the Prussians coming back from a military exercise rang out below our windows. Mr Hamel stood up, very pale, at his desk. Never had he seemed so tall.*

"My friends", he said, "my friends, I . . . I . . ."

But something seemed to stifle him. He was unable to complete his sentence.

Then he turned to the blackboard, picked up a piece of chalk, and, pressing as hard as he could, he wrote as big as possible:

VIVE LA FRANCE!

* * *

Occupation came again in 1940, and the Germans made renewed efforts to bring Alsace again to its German culture. Again in vain, in spite of (or maybe because of) that concentration camp set up in the Vosges, high up at Let Struthof. Liberation came in the winter of 1944/5, though not without some heavy fighting round pockets of German resistance about Strasbourg and Colmar.

Now, although Strasbourg is the home of the Council of Europe, one of the main centres of the Common Market, and a European city rather than a French one, although its port handles great volumes of freight, Alsace itself remains, basically, what it always was, a single-minded, simple trading region, independent, with its own dialect and attitudes, and financially at least closely linked with France.

The spread of the plain, with its fertile "*loess*"-based soil, demands total obedience from the land-workers, and the industries that derive from the land offer steady jobs, more secure jobs at present than those of the old manufacturing and mining areas, where the future is somewhat uncertain. On the whole, though, it is a prosperous country, but the very number of the opportunities that spring from its geographical position at the hub of the E.E.C. countries creates local anxieties and doubts.

In a way this is a product of the past. During the long period of the alien occupation from 1870 to 1918, many Alsatian industries were either transplanted to other parts of France or were closed down by the occupiers in order to remove competition from their home-grown resources. It has already been pointed out that only one rail link with France existed before 1918. Even when that situation had been improved after 1918, investment was slow to return to Alsace because of natural fears about the future of the province. It is only recently, after the last War, that much has been done to promote industrial growth. Really only Strasbourg gained from the Prussian occupation: the vast complex of its port was planned and basically constructed at that time, though it has, naturally, been greatly enlarged since.

The great plain has a character all of its own. Nowhere else looks quite like this, quite flat as far as the foothills of the mountains, squared into wide patches of cultivation, tilled and tilled until you feel that not a square inch has been left fallow. Wheat, rye and barley are elbowed out by sweet corn, hops, tobacco, and there is often a small vineyard at the edge of fields or at the back of a house. Higgledy-piggledy buildings, disorganised except where Vauban's military logic, as at Neuf-Brisach, has imposed French rationalism, mostly with very tall and steep roofs, often with dormers or tiny half-closed eyes of windows tucked into them. The usual style of building, there being no stone on the plain, is lath and plaster, or brick and rubble strengthened by plaster and enclosed by fat black beams, upper storeys pressing outwards on the primitive cantilever of joists and beams. The woodwork is often lavishly carved, as in that splendid house in the main street of Saverne, or the Kammerzell house by the cathedral of Strasbourg, or many others in Colmar and village after village. The walls are frequently painted with religious pictures, as in the Pfister house in Colmar or the Town Hall in Mulhouse. In the south, especially, the roof tiles are coloured in geometrical patterns, and then varnished, very lively and decorative. Balconies everywhere and masses of flowers in them. They believe in colour to welcome the summer after a long and savage winter. The legendary storks, however, have virtually disappeared, leaving only the odd nest carefully preserved, for luck, for a memorial, or to appeal to the tourist. Wrought iron-work is widespread and adds its sweet lines and fantasy to this world of fairy-tales.

The Rhine has always dominated the area. Control a crossing place and your fortune was made. But the Rhine has always been a wilful river, as wilful as the Alsatian, and it has never been content to keep to one established bed. The land is so flat that flooding has, over the centuries, been a constant threat. The waywardness of this great waterway, too, has tended to make navigation on it a difficult matter.

In 1928, by an act of far-sighted confidence, the French Government launched a scheme to harness the Rhine and to tame it. This was a major piece of construction work. From the Swiss border down to the region of Strasbourg the river's level drops rapidly, making navigation even more difficult. Another element in the decision to build a great canal beside the river was the constant preoccupation with hydro-electric schemes. Thus the situation was considered ideal for the launching of what had to be a highly costly construction programme which has continued even more rapidly since the end of the last War.

The canal itself is very wide, 100 to 130 metres, and at each level-change there are paired locks served by hydraulically operated gates. Dams across the river provide the necessary flow of water. The power-stations are constructed over 'slipways' which control the input of water required by the locks. This head of water is converted into electrical energy, and this is distributed via locally sited high voltage step-down stations to various substations throughout the region. The total energy thus created makes a great contribution to the energy requirements of eastern France. Work is now in hand for a Franco-German installation downstream of Strasbourg.

The canal carries a tremendous volume of freight both to and from Alsace. The main industries of this area include textiles, potash and potassium products, oil refining, timber, and paper, and, in the North, glass. The main interest, however, lies probably in food and drink. The local dishes tend to be Germanic in type, from Strasbourg *foie-gras*, to sausage and sauerkraut (or *choucroute*) which are all produced in quantity.

Wine and beer are both produced and consumed mightily, very good wine and very good beer. Along the lower slopes of the main bank of the Vosges, especially towards the south, the whole countryside is one vineyard, or so it seems. Apart from the large acres cultivated by big growers or large communes, every little garden seems to have its postage-stamp plantation. Most of the wines are white and similar to hock or Moselle. There are a number of local names over whose merits the experts argue. The answer for the amateur is to go and sample the various wines for him- or herself. All are splendid after a little experience. Beer, mostly a good lager, comes in many brews and, although not "good British bitter", is excellent of its type.

What is pleasant to find, at least for British visitors, is the sort of café, that exists in Alsatian towns. There is almost a 'pub' atmosphere there not usually found in France. You see the regulars coming in each with the russet cheeks of the true beer drinker. They sit together at their usual tables, ageing gentlemen in dark clothes, white-haired and with handlebar moustaches and hats or berets, and settle down for the evening just as their counterparts in England do. It is almost like home!

8. The Middle Vosges

The blue line of the Vosges is the constant backdrop against which the life of Alsace is played out. The mountains run continuously down along the western horizon like a giant gallery overlooking the humble activities of the human players, and they gradually get higher the nearer they approach the Alps. Not that they try to vie with the Alps; they are placid and maternal in their build and character, a world for walkers, not climbers.

The highest heights rise to something over 4,500 feet, but the rise is gradual and the shapes are mainly rotund, not pointed. As you go south in spring, little by little a few more flecks of snow appear beside the road, or the trees thin out to leave the wide open grasslands, fine, springy turf, which are the '*chaumes*', the high pastures, in summer. These highlands are not unlike the South Downs, except that they are much, much higher. The shape is the same, rounded, grass-covered tors, and it is not surprising they are called '*ballons*' or '*Kopfe*'.

The valleys leading up to these heights have their industries, mostly small works, even cottage activities, timber, carpentry, fish-breeding, a bit of weaving to make the colourful local cloths and aprons, pottery, wine, cheese, especially that soft, crusted and very odoriferous cheese known as '*munster*'. On one occasion we tried to bring some back to England. We soon realised why it never appeared in our shops; no one could possibly transport it! It is something else you really have to go to the Vosges to savour, and it is a haunting experience. Gradually, too, the tourist and winter sports trades are growing; ski-runs show up among the trees, and lakes and valley sites are sprouting caravans and tents. The Vosges have come late to this game, but, alas, their popularity is increasing fast as more people come to appreciate the area. This is superb holiday country, still relatively unspoiled and unsophisticated. Expect no night spots, no cultivated après-ski, no international cuisine up here in the heights. But you can still breathe pure air, walk in vast pine forests, look down on tiny villages and escape, if you wish from your fellow men.

There are so many castles topping the hills, or rather so many towers, turrets, piles of stones, that it is impossible to list them all. Those we think the best and most interesting have their place here, but others are so remote or so dilapidated that they are necessarily omitted.

Just south of Saverne, the valley of the Zorn has, through history carried the main traffic routes through the Col and down to Strasbourg. Near Arzviller the Marne-Rhine canal has to make its way up a strenuous last 100 feet. Since 1969 it has been equipped with a massive barge-elevator, a metal trough that is hauled up, as another goes down, an inclined plane, thus transporting the large barges that constantly use this route. In the past there was a system of 17 locks over the same climb, and the process used to take a whole day to accomplish. The modern barge-lift makes the move in 20 minutes.

South again, along the D.45, you climb over the watershed into the valley of the Grossthal and so into the little town of Dabo, whose rock still supports the remnants, little more than a chapel and tower, of the ancient castle of the Dabo (or Dagsbourg) family. This clan was descended from Duke Etichon, one of those 7th century robber barons who later, like Gérard d'Alsace, became respectable. Etichon established a powerful authority over this part of the country. He appears again in our history in his castle of Obernai as the father of Saint Odile, and other descendants turn up in various pages of Alsatian medieval records.

One of the Dabo branch became famous, both in fact and legend, as Pope Leo IX, later Saint Leo. That is fact. The legend, carefully preserved in folk-lore and children's tales, is that, not unlike Dick Whittington, he was led to Rome by the cry of the cockerels along the way, who called out to him: '*Leo Papa*'. Did the birds only echo his own aspirations, or did they know a thing or two? Anyway he was the last Dabo to get more than a brief mention in any history book, and the family disappeared in the 17th century. When Louis

View from Quarry at Le Struthof

XIV finally obtained control of Alsace the Dabos were not, it seems, quick enough to kiss the royal boot. Their castle was captured by French troops in 1677, and the building was destroyed two years later. It is somehow sad to see them pass out of history. But that is the story of the majority of old families – their gradual emasculation, the disappearance of the name into the female line, or their annihilation because of a wrong choice in the loyalty game.

The whole of this uncrowded area is fine for walking or even some gentle climbing. A little further south, for instance, is Nideck, offering castle and water-falls. There is nothing easy about visiting either. At best they require quite a walk, at worst a frustrating search along a maze of paths inadequately (or, in at least one case, over-adequately) marked. The key-point is the '*Maison Forestière du Nideck*' on the D.218 between Wangenbourg and Oberhaslach. Opposite the Maison is a car-park of sorts and from there a longish path leads either to the Falls or to the Castle, or to both if you like. The path divides after a short distance, and is marked by a bewildering multiplicity of signs. However, if you bear right you arrive at the remains of the castle, just two towers, the higher of which has some terrifying steps to the top, more terrifying as you come down because you seem to tread outwards into sheer space, and the handrail is worse than rickety. The view is superb. Fork left lower down on the path and you reach the Falls that tumble richly over their porphyry base. These can also be reached from lower down on

Obernai

the D.218 by starting at the *Hôtel de la Cascade*, if you succeed in choosing the right path! Nearby is the Schneeberg at a little over 2,800 feet, if you are keen on hill-walking.

From Nideck the mountains slope down to the valley of the Bruche, by which a second rail link now winds its way across to St-Dié and the West. This valley is broad, luxuriant in its lower levels, with occasional small industrial concerns, metal-working, machine-rools, textiles, saw-mills, fish-farming. The road becomes steeper as it rises from Schirmeck up on to the Col of Donon. This also goes down to St-Dié, another sad town that was almost burned to the ground by the retreating Germans. Even the cathedral was blown up. Not very much remains now, alas, to attract the tourist.

As you go up towards the top of the Col du Donon, the great woods of beeches and firs open out on the fine open pastures of the highlands. A good walking area, the Col offers wide expanses of views to the eye of the car-borne. Down in the valleys are attractive villages, toy-size, like Grandfontaine with its tall, very white church and fish-ponds. From here it is only a short drive to the region of the '*Hochwald*', the High Forest.

If you go that way, along the D.130, you will pass a grim reminder of the last War. There, at Le Struthof, during the Nazi occupation a concentration camp was established. It was built by prisoners up on this bitter corner of the high hills. The granite was quarried there in dreadful conditions of cold and starvation, and was carried to make the roads and the terracing for the barrack-blocks. Life expectancy in these conditions was short, and this was in part, at least, the intention; the victims, many of them French, were sent here to die.

There was also a small gas chamber, still preserved, to which selected groups of victims were sent, and there is, set out there, a poignant description of the death of the first 20 women, sent there from Auschwitz and whose bodies were returned to the doctor at Auschwitz for post-mortem examination, these women being, presumably, used for some special experimentation. The description is the more poignant because it is in the callous words of the Camp Commandant himself.

Some 10,000 people died here, either gassed or as a result of the bitter cold and the heavy labour in the quarries, and much of the camp is preserved as a memorial to them. There is also a strange concrete structure, curved and pointed, that juts into the sky as a more specific, but incomprehensible, memorial.

From there the road leads in gentle slopes up to the arête that is topped by the tower of the *Champ de Feu* (Field of Fire). Here the forest has mostly slipped away, and this upland plain is fairly bare. The road, an old military road, runs along the ridge, and from the top of the tower (up 105 steps), on its somewhat dilapidated roof, there opens out an enormous view over Strasbourg to the Black Forest, and the line of the humps of the higher, southern Vosges striding away down to Switzerland.

Down below, on the eastern side, the ancient spread of castles, abbeys, vineyards, weinstube and tourists continues. Go down the D.57, a magnificent *corniche* road filled with grand views, and on to the D.426 through Le Hochwald village, a popular resort for seekers of peace, and so to the Convent of Saint Odile.

It stands on a forward spur of the hills, staring out over the plain. The hill, it seems, was used as a defensive stronghold by early peoples, perhaps the Celts. They raised a wall, an immense wall, to enclose an area big enough, surely, to contain the whole existing population of Alsace. It was over 6 miles long and probably over 6 feet high. It is known as the Pagan Wall, and the great blocks of stone, still standing here and there, are startling in their size.

But it is not for this '*Mur Païen*' that tourists flock here in their thousands; it is to visit the convent itself.

Odile was the daughter of the Duke Etichon we have already met. She was born in the ducal residence in Obernai, down under the protection of the Hohenbourg castle on the hill behind the town. Unfortunately she was born blind and sickly. The Duke wanted a son so he ordered her to be killed. She was saved by her nurse and later became a Christian. When all this was revealed to the father, he set to work to hunt her down. She was saved by a miracle, a crag opening to allow her to escape from him. Etichon himself was converted by her, and gave her the castle of Hohenbourg. It was beside it that she founded her convent.

For several centuries, the convent enjoyed great prosperity, both as the centre of a widespread cult of the Saint and as one of the religious houses favoured by the unworldly and unmarried daughters of noble families. In the 16th century, however, as the result of the combined attacks of a destructive fire and the inroads of heresy, the convent disintegrated and the nuns were dispersed. It was not until 1853 that the Bishop of Strasbourg re-established it as a convent.

Not much of the early buildings now stands, of course. Only the Chapelle de la Croix, a basically Romanesque structure, which, with the tiny chapelle Ste-Odile, that stands next to it joined by a low door, and in which the remains of the Saint are lying in an ancient stone sarcophagus, are the original relics of the convent. Otherwise the buildings are a hotch-potch of later architecture and are really rather dull. From the terrace there is a fine view, and a short distance down the hill is the spring brought about miraculously by the Saint to quench the thirst of an old man. He had brought his blind child for her to cure, and those with eye troubles still come to this spring to find a cure for their affliction. The mass of people who come to the convent may be divided into the devout, seeking miracles, the tour addicts, and the school parties who find the ice-cream as much to their taste here as anywhere else. From the road to Obernai there are some impressive views of the convent standing imposingly on its crag.

Obernai is another magnificent example of ancient Alsatian town, all beams and tall, sharp gables. The narrow streets snake and wind, and are swamped by cars. The old town walls still stand, or parts of them still stand, even the remnants of watch-towers. Within their framework there is a treasury of fine buildings, the old corn market of 1554, the Town Hall, a restored 16th century building with a grand balcony, and, behind it, the 13th century bell-tower of a destroyed chapel, and the highly recommended *Hôtel Le Parc*. Not far off is a beautiful ornate well of 1579 which could handle six

Molsheim – The Metzig

buckets simultaneously. All these are in, or near, the Place du Marché, which is all surrounded by ancient buildings in that dark red sandstone that gives the place its individuality, and, in some lights, its rather sinister air.

Not far away is the Place de l'Etoile, too, striking in its array of age-old houses and the delightful flowered decoration that gives it personality and vividness. Somehow this little square, less pretentious, perhaps, than the Market Square, has more of a feeling of daily use, of reality even. This, too, can be felt in the shops and the bars and cafés which are full of locals, weatherbeaten, rugged men in dark clothes, sitting and smoking their pipes, obvious regulars, men of character and country pride. This is not a town that is geared to stripping the tourist of his cash. It is a fine and matey place. The tourists pass through in their hordes and hardly seem to affect the inhabitants.

Almost due north of Obernai is a small place that deserves a mention and a visit. Molsheim is a neat, compact, closely knit town that has hardly yet overstepped the bounds set by its old walls. Not that much of them still stands, a few stones only and a town gate.

What attracts interest and admiration is the Metzig, a lovely and shapely building that was the Headquarters of the Butchers' Guild and built for them in the 16th century. The first floor is really one large meeting hall. Two graceful staircases lead up to it from the town's main square, and come together in a small balcony under an ornate belfry. The roof rises steeply to a great height and contains two further floors under it and its great triangular walls are flamboyantly decorated with sinuous and stepped gable ends. Round these walls, at the first floor level run balconies with finely carved balustrades. The essential business of the butchers was carried on in the recesses behind the arches of the ground floor. This space is now occupied by a wine-tasting cellar.

In this square, surrounded by the inevitable mass of parked cars, is a fine Renaissance fountain that proudly displays the town's coat of arms borne by a lion.

Although good wine is grown around here, most of the terrain is given up to even better beer. This is the hop area, and several big, and highly modern, breweries can be seen. Mutzig, not far away, gives its name to one of the principal brews. If there were a "*Route des Bières*" it would pass through here, and so on to Strasbourg.

9. Strasbourg

Trade created, and trade has maintained, Strasbourg. It stands not on the banks of the Rhine, which, until engineers tackled the problem during the last century, had the habit of shifting its course, to the danger of anything in its way, but on an island formed by the two arms of the river Ill. This gave it a strong defensive position, further strengthened by fortifications. The city walls were enlarged and thickened as the Middle Ages developed more and more powerful offensive weapons. The only relics now of the medieval bastions are the walled bridges, known rather curiously as the '*ponts couverts*', sheltered perhaps, but hardly covered, by four massive towers.

In the first century B.C., the town of '*Argentoratum*', as the Romans named it, grew up on the crossroads of trading routes, commanding a possible crossing-place of the Rhine and near enough to the Col de Saverne for that easy route over the Vosges. The Rhine traffic developed within the protective framework of the Holy Roman Empire. This town, now *Strass-burg*, the "town of the roads", developed with it. In 1336 it was granted the right to hold a great Imperial Fair, its Bishops became Princes of the Empire, and, by the 15th century, it had its own municipal bank. By 1596 it had 25,000 inhabitants, a magnificent cathedral and a host of fine, luxurious houses, of which a fair number still exist. These show how the city was bursting at its island seams, because they are tall and narrow; the physical pressures of space that created skyscrapers

Strasbourg – Old Houses

were at work here. Only the technical know-how was lacking. They built as high as they could, lacking girders or even stone. The old business quarters of Petite France, St-Etienne, the quays of the '*Bateliers*' and the '*Pêcheurs*' still give a memorable picture of the way life must have been lived in the late Middle Ages, and the old houses are still in use for the purpose for which they were built, as offices, dwellings, bars, restaurants, and they are still an important part of the social life of the city today. The town has fine restaurants notably the *Buerehiesel*, the *Crocodile* and the *Au Gourmet* and *Sans Chique*.

Strasbourg accepts its old buildings as normal features of everyday life; there is no sense of artificial preservation, of showmanship, of twee-ness, the sort of clucking titivation you find in Ribeauvillé or Haut-Koenigsberg. In Strasbourg the old exists side by side with, and is judged in comparison with, the new, and frequently comes off best as being more efficient as well as more sightly. You have only to look at the gimcrack and tawdry new Council of Europe building and then go again to look at the Palace of the Rohan family to

Strasbourg – Council of Europe Building

appreciate what this means. The former, with its reinforced concrete structure covered over in precast cladding units in a milk-chocolate colour in odd angles, with a mass of coffee-coloured mirror-glass windows bulging out in great, unnatural shelves, presents a pointless, shapeless mass of illogical facets. The Palace of the Rohans, built in the early 18th century, may, on the other hand, seem unduly austere with its precise ranges of similar and mathematically conceived windows, its Corinthian columns, its pediment and sheer size, along the frontage that faces the river, but it is coherent, impressive, absolutely logical and adapted to its required function, *une Rolls-Royce à habiter*!

* * *

Strasbourg now is probably more European than French, or even Alsatian. It stands somewhere near the geographical centre of the Common Market countries. The links with Germany, especially since the construction of the great, sweeping Pont de l'Europe, are

Strasbourg – Kammerzell House

Strasbourg – Cathedral Tower dominates the City

as strong as those with France; peace and de Gaulle's policies have almost achieved what years of occupation failed to establish. Strasbourg is a cosmopolitan city, but a proud and a wealthy one.

The centre, surely, is the Cathedral, itself strangely independent in style, and its asymmetrical front, visible from all parts of Alsace, even from the most distant pinnacles of the northern Vosges, is known to every Alsatian and is a standing symbol of the province. It is built of Vosges sandstone, red, often blood-red in colour, and the west front is an enormous, solid mass of masonry some 150 feet high. On one side of this a tall and powerful tower has been raised, only one, topped by a spire, the whole about 320 feet in height, a massive piece of building that stands up like a giant L and peers out aggressively over the plain, staring into Germany. It is as unbending, defiant and individualistic as the Alsatian himself. It is possible to go up to the high platform of the façade and enjoy the tremendous view, not only of the surrounding countryside but of the city itself.

The interior has to be seen; there is nothing quite like it anywhere else, not just because it is an architectural triumph or even a model of architectural style, but because it is a fairyland of colour and space and light. Like the rest of the building, it is all of different periods and schools, from Romanesque through various phases of the Gothic. There are some magnificent medieval statues and a fascinating astronomical clock with a multitude of dials, figures and every sort of astronomical information, Death strikes the hours and the four Ages of Man strike the quarters, with angels in attendance and always something to watch. It is, in fact, a 19th century reconstruction of an earlier clock.

The real joy of the building, for me at least, is the stained glass, absolutely marvellous medieval colouring of splendidly simple medieval messages. These windows were taken out during the last War and stored away in France until the Occupation forces removed them to Germany. At the end they were discovered by American troops deep in a salt mine in Würtenburg. Look at the fearful Devil in the first window on the right, herding his collection of souls into Hell. There must once have been a companion representation of the saved souls in Heaven, but this, perhaps symbolically, seems to have been lost. Further along is a sort of strip version of the Crucifixion, the story running from left to right and beginning at the bottom. The small east window over the main altar is modern, a gallant attempt to match the originals but, for all that, a failure; the colouring lacks the depth and richness of the medieval craftsmen. The great rose window at the west end, however, is a superb mass of gorgeous colouring.

Outside, the vast, ornate west front is a fine example of 13th century sculpture, though here and there some more recent workmanship, necessitated by revolutionary damage and war shows a less interesting style. The three lower lines of statuary where the tale of the Crucifixion and Resurrection is told, especially the topmost of the three where Judas hangs himself and monsters are released from Hell, have great vitality and realism. The top line, of the

Strasbourg – Place Kléber

Ascension, is more modern. All in all, the whole front is vivid and exciting, its lines soaring upwards towards the single finger of the tower pointing to heaven.

In other cities this west front would dominate the environs much more than it does here. In a way it is too enormous to be taken in at a glance and the space is too cramped; what is lacking is the long view across a big square as at, say, Notre-Dame in Paris. As well as that, the surroundings themselves hold the eye, old, timbered houses, the deep red brick and decorated black coffee beams of the Kammerzell House just beside the Cathedral, the narrow streets that give just a glimpse of the great tower, the Place du Château with the front of the Rohan mansion behind its gates that open on to the main courtyard, the medieval Museum of Cathedral Treasures, and all the wrought ironwork and the baskets and troughs full of flowers. Everywhere you look in this city you are fascinated by the wealth of beauty and the richness of history, and it is not a museum – this cannot be stressed too much – it is lived in and it functions in the world of today.

* * *

If you look down on the great expanse of Strasbourg from the platform of the Cathedral, you can see how the steep ridges of old roofs, gathered hugger-mugger beneath the protection of Notre-Dame, spread out through later and lighter buildings, even slate covered some of them, to the modern symmetry of concrete in the carefully engineered suburbs of today. It all seems to fit together like some haphazard jigsaw. The same is true of the Place Kléber, the Piccadilly Circus of Strasbourg. The historical range of the buildings here is vast, from the crushed and etiolated medieval with pinched and pinnacled roofs through every age and style, all harmonised and blended into coherence, and all of them surrounding what is now little more than a large underground car park. The empty middle space of the square is used for all sorts of pleasant and useful things. Last time we were there, it held a kiddies' merry-go-round, as well as considerable space set aside for bicycles and mopeds for the use of the young of the city, a mark of the attention paid to the comfort and welfare of the youngsters. The Place Kléber is beautiful, rather jolly and very, very elegant.

It is difficult, in a book like this, to describe in detail, all the places that should be seen. Strasbourg is a city to wander in, certainly not to drive in – that is hell! – and to take in very slowly, like an old cognac.

Museum addicts and lovers of art will surely linger for a long time in and around the Place du Château just outside the south walls of the Cathedral. There in the Rohan palace and in the Museum of the Cathedral treasures are set out. In the medieval and Renaissance houses next door are several fine exhibitions. Medieval ecclesiastical sculpture is lavishly displayed in the latter rooms. Perhaps the most interesting exhibit, however, is what is probably the oldest stained glass window to represent a human figure in existence, the "Head of Christ" from Wissembourg. In the Rohan château there are several displays, all based on the family collections. Painting is well represented and includes a glorious El Greco of the Virgin of Sorrows. But there are also furniture, porcelain and documents and prints.

The house itself is probably best seen from the river, where the frontage overwhelms by its size and cool efficiency. Across the river

Strasbourg – Quai des Bateliers

the street is lined by fine town houses of the seventeenth and eighteenth centuries, another example of the elegance and completeness of the city. If you turn right after crossing the river, you come to the Place du Corbeau. There you can go under the square-topped archway of No 1, which is part of the premises of Ott Frères, who deal in ecclesiastical fittings, and you immediately find yourself in the 14th century. Carefully preserved inside is the large yard of the old Corbeau Inn, once the main posting house of Strasbourg, where, over the centuries, lodged many of the notables of France. It is a long area, with balcony all round, a bridge linking the two halves of the inn over the middle, dark staircases, and still in use, either as flats or offices. It gives a good, and somehow eerie impression of what it must once have been like in its heyday.

The Pont Corbeau, nearby, leads back to the city. This is a place of ancient horror. Here were carried out the fearsome sentences pronounced on infanticides and parricides. Those found guilty were incarcerated in iron cages and immersed in the river until drowned. Across the river is the rebuilt municipal customs house in whose

Strasbourg – Petite France

warehouses once were stored the dutiable goods brought in by river transport. Largely destroyed at the end of the last War, it was rebuilt in 1965, and is a museum of Alsatian life and folklore.

Round this area were the old city markets, for meat, fish, sucking pigs, grain. These occupied the little squares that suddenly appear as you walk, surrounded, mostly, by the ancient houses once lived in by the traders themselves.

Follow the river round upstream and soon you find yourself in the Middle Ages, in the narrow streets that belonged to the old trades and professions, in La Petite France and the Tanners' quarter, where the houses lean out over the streets, upper storeys resting on wooden props, gables stretching down and jutting forward aggressively, ancient timbers, decoratively modelled and arranged, still supporting bulging façades. Here and there they are repeated exactly in the channelled waters of the Ill. Little bridges cross from point to point and the whole place has more right to be called "*little Venice*" than many other towns and areas that arrogate to themselves that name. Just beyond are the square towers of the *Ponts*

Couverts and then the dam, grass-topped, set there by Vauban to defend the city and France. This gives a fine view of the old quarters and seems to place the tower of the Cathedral above them in a sort of protective pose.

These magnificent houses of the end of the sixteenth century mark the culmination of Strasbourg's medieval power and wealth. It was not for another century that such luxury and sheer *joie de vivre* were to reappear, and then the circumstances, even the government, were quite changed.

That intervening century was one of storm and stress, of bitterness and destruction. First, at the end of the 16th century, had come the evils of religious intolerance; acrimony had flared, and families and friends torn apart. There was no escaping the infection, and trade suffered along with the old sense of co-operation and mutual prosperity. Despite the moves of the Council of Trent and the efforts of the Hapsburg rulers, Protestantism carried the day over much of the Rhineland, including Strasbourg, where even the Cathedral was taken over by the new faith. It was not until 1681, when French rule was finally established, that it was restored to the Roman Church.

The disruption of life due to religious struggles was followed soon after by the desolation of the Thirty Years War, itself, in its origin, largely the product of that same battle for men's souls, or at least allegiance, the Protestant German Princes versus the Catholic Emperor. Even to describe it like that is to simplify what certainly became a war for political advantage, in which France became involved because of the machiavellian Cardinal Richelieu who believed he could extract a few valuable acres for France.

War hurts everyone perhaps, but it damages most the little people, the Mother Courage folk over whose land and livelihood it passes. The whole Rhineland was at stake in this bitter war, and armies then lived off the land. Strasbourg stood upon the obvious crossing-place of the Rhine for invasion or just simply for spoils.

So, for these two causes, the City of the Roads suffered for something like a hundred years. Little progress was, or could be, made in this time; the population remained static; plague followed the soldiery; misery had to be borne. Only in 1678 was the warring brought to an end. Strasbourg was not included in the settlement that concluded the war, but this did not deter Louis XIV. France had been awarded most of the principal cities of Alsace, thus bringing to fruition Richelieu's reasons for involvement in the war, but Strasbourg was a free city, its freedom guaranteed by both the

Emperor and France, to whom she owed some nominal loyalty. Using that situation to his advantage, and being quite sure that no one would be prepared to relight the flames of war just for one city, Louis assumed control of it and appointed a governor. His thinking proved correct, and so, from 1681, Strasbourg was French.

* * *

This event led to a period of renewed splendour, of which the Rohan house of 1704 is the supreme testimony. Other wealthy people, too, soon set out to build themselves town houses and palaces worthy of their social position. The Joneses of that community all had hyphenated names and titles. They built mainly to the north of the city in what are now the rue du Dôme and the other streets around the Place Broglie, all of which provide a continuous lesson in the stylised and perfect engineers' architecture of the Age of Reason. The Town Hall and the Prefecture are good examples of the style, all cool, massive, perfectly proportioned, nothing like the traditional Alsatian buildings, but fully in line with the arrogance of pre-Revolutionary France.

Cross the river from the Place Broglie to the Place de la République and you are immediately in a different world, architecturally speaking. In an effort to create their own centre for this city, the German occupiers of 1871 tried to move the Administration, and so the heart, to this part. Here stands the Imperial Palace in good, solid Prussian style, lifeless, cumbersome, but imposing. The square itself is huge, with a grand circular garden in the middle. The Germanic influence stretches out to the east and south, with wide streets and square-cut crossroads, out towards the very pleasant Orangery gardens, originally by Le Nôtre, the designer of the Versailles gardens, and put into order again in 1804 in preparation for a stay here by the Empress Josephine. Now it is a popular resort of old people and young lovers.

Out then into a further circle of development, that of international Strasbourg, with its gross Council of Europe building and the much more successful Palais des Expositions, a charming and efficient design, almost certainly wholly French; it has balance and order and meaning.

Of course it is money that created Strasbourg, and it is money that has preserved and made usable these relics of the past that make up La Petite France and the area round the Corbeau Inn or the Place Kléber. Everywhere you go the old shells are being remoulded and repaired inside, just as most of our own picturesque village streets, half-timbered frontages and thatch cloak the cocktail bar and the split-level homes that are in vogue today. That doesn't matter. Changes and reconstructions have doubtless been carried out throughout the ages. What does matter is that the buildings are still used. That gives them validity as living things.

A lot of Strasbourg's money comes from transportation, and the centre of that is to the east of the city where the Rhine has, in all history, carried the trade. Since the construction of the great Rhine canal and the taming of the river, this trade has increased enormously and very large barges can travel up and down to the North Sea and to Basle. The port of Strasbourg is a very large complex of docks that has grown up over a wide area and over a long period of time. It is still the crossroads of Western Europe of several lines of transportation, a junction that handles a vast trade in manufactured goods, minerals and cereals for the region in which it stands. In 1970 the port handled 12.3 megatonnes, of which by far the greatest part was in exports, mainly gravel and other building materials, with hydrocarbons a close second in the list. Over half the working people of the area have their employment somewhere in this port complex. So the port of Strasbourg is an enormous element in the economy of the city, and this is a case of history, by constant change and modernisation, becoming today.

In and about Strasbourg there is something to appeal to every interest or any taste. There is something particularly pleasant about the affable citizens, the lively young people, the mostly welcoming hôteliers, often housed in ancient premises. There are a great number of hotels, of course, at every price, and there are two good camp sites for the money-savers; the *Montagne-Verte* is adequate and very convenient, only just outside the city centre on the N.392 road south, and the other, grander, is at *Baggersee*, off the N.68. Good hotel accommodation can be found in the town, at the *Hôtel Châteaulinard*, or less expensively, at the *Hôstellerie Riss*, in nearby Lampertheim.

10. La Route des Vins

Although the so-called Route des Vins, established of course to attract visitors to the *caves*, or tasting rooms, of the various wine-producing centres along the way, starts just south of Wasselonne, the main wine-growing area really begins further down, below Obernai. From there it runs down, along the lower slopes of the Vosges, as far as Guebwiller or even Thann, with the greatest concentration of vineyards and the most important products to be found near the centre of that region that lies between Ribeauvillé and Ammerschwihr. Whether you are wine-conscious or not hardly matters; the road takes you through some lovely villages and towns.

Along these eastern slopes of the mountains, the vineyards are sheltered, benefit from a dry climate and find a well-drained soil on the sandstone beds or gravels. It is because of this that the main growing areas are seldom to be found right down on the plain, though small plantations do appear there. These are of small importance and are probably a relic of the German occupation prior to 1918, when the new rulers expanded considerably the area devoted to wine production to satisfy the voracious thirsts of the Fatherland, and also to ensure that Alsatian wine should never compete at least in quality with the wines produced on the other side of the Rhine.

Wine has been grown here since time immemorial. Romans, as usual, planted their vines as soon as they came. Later, monasteries and castles established their sources of supply of the necessities of life. Cities and towns, as they grew in power and wealth, soon followed suit. Then the villages united and laid down group rights and organised the plots of land so as to ensure fair shares for all of the good and bad soils. Dealers quickly appeared to take advantage of the flow of wine, to dispose of, and, if need be, to process, the crop. More recently village co-operatives have been developed with success and profit to the members.

The hillsides, covered with huge sweeps of vines in plots lined up in different directions, present at the various seasons an eye-catching design, like the hatching of some abstract etching. Lines of gaunt stumps in spring, green avenues in summer, swarming carrier-ants of the pickers in October. There is a curious fascination about their shape.

The wine villages and townships, prosperous through their products, are mostly places of great charm, even beauty. The fifteenth and sixteenth century houses are often large and luxurious, notably, of course, those built by the *négociants*. The old inns, too, are especially fine. Medieval war-makers were usually careful not to destroy vineyards; after all, what is the point of capturing a place if, in the process, you destroy the source of its wealth? The villages, therefore, at least up to 1944, were left alone to produce their nectar. They took their own precautions, of course, and most of them have their fortifications, some, as at Riquewihr, Dambach, Eguisheim and Bergheim, for example, of considerable strength.

The long German Occupation, concentrating on quantity rather than quality, and the devastating outbreak of the phylloxera disease around the turn of the century had together led to a debasement of the Alsatian wine products. It has required a long and careful husbandry to bring the industry to the high standards of today, when the best wines, the fine Rieslings, Traminers and Gewurtztraminers, the drier Sylvaners and the Alsatian Muscats, enjoy a world-wide reputation.

If you follow the whole Route des Vins, along which you can, of course, sample the local specialities, the word '*dégustation*' (tasting) appears everywhere, you will perhaps end up regretting your indulgence or, alternatively, surfeited with the sight of vines and the beauties of Alsatian architecture. Although, therefore, for convenience, we have kept to the Route, we would urge you to take it in small measures!

Southwards from Obernai, the first village to catch the eye is Dambach-la-Ville because the town walls are in very good condition. The three gates, too, with their towers still keep watch and ward there. Inside it is a beautiful place, fully medieval with fif-

Turckheim – Among its Vineyards

teenth and sixteenth century houses, balconied and laden with flowers. Beams are carved and the houses stepped outwards over the street. A good place to visit.

On the other hand, the bigger town of Sélestat, with the best will in the world, can only be described as 'dull'. It has two old churches, both considerably restored and rebuilt at various times and for various reasons, and very little else except a most imposing water tower.

Going on southwards from here, the eye is certainly held by the castle of Haut-Köenigsberg up on the hill above St-Hippolyte. In fact it is so eye-catching that it appears on the cover of most of the books or pamphlets (even maps!) about Alsace. There is not even a photograph of it here! And this for the good reason that it is almost all a 20th century fabrication! Certainly the ancient foundations of a magnificent castle were used as the basis for the construction, and something of the original fortress, an enormous one belonging to a family of Swiss counts and burnt to the ground by the Swedish forces employed in the Thirty Years War, can be seen. The present work was carried out in the early years of this century at the orders of Wilhelm II of Germany. The resultant structure is probably more imposing than the earlier one largely because of the massiveness of the fortifications, especially the huge square keep that replaces the earlier round one. It is a very popular tourist attraction, and you have to go round it in guided groups, a circumstance that never really appeals to me.

* * *

Bergheim is often neglected, but the remaining town walls with a good gate and a square tower with its dunce's cap on top, all of the 14th century, together with its flower-decked Market Square, give it an appeal that makes the very short detour worth while.

There are more castles per square mile hereabouts than anywhere else in the province, built there presumably because of the importance of the vineyards down below. The number of these strongholds is so absurd that it almost seems that there must have been a big trade in them, a sort of castle-development organisation created by some medieval entrepreneur. '*Desirable strongholds for sale in luxury development. Mountain scenery. Not overlooked*'. Or does that suggestion lack proper deference?

Ribeauvillé has one fine hotel, the *Clos St-Vincent* and no less than three ruined fortresses on the hills above it. They were, in fact, separate establishments of the same powerful family, that of Ribeaupierre. One of them, the best preserved, that of St Ulrich, stands as if lined up deliberately with the main street that straggles up a gentle slope towards it, between its timber-framed houses and shops. Ribeauvillé is a place of ancient buildings and ancient customs. The main '*jour de fête*' here is held on the last Sunday in August. It is, or rather was, a musical occasion held in praise of their Lord of Ribeaupierre who, as their liege lord, some time in the distant past, granted them corporate rights that were later recognised by the French Council of Colmar. This festival is called *Pfiffertag* (Pipers' Day) or *Fête des Ménétriers* (Musicians' Festival). Originally this was a sort of Eisteddfodd or the musical part of a Highland Games, to which the local musicians all came to compete with each other. Naturally it was also a wine festival, a libation to the gods of wine to try to ensure a good harvest. Now there is a procession, not much musical competition, but a lot of free wine, which certainly attracts the visitors from far and near. So much so that there is also a sort of dress rehearsal at the end of July, a huge wine fair.

Even more, perhaps, than the excellent wine produced here, the tourist trade has become the *raison d'être* of Ribeauvillé. And yet, not so long ago, the place was one of the bastions of liberty and French independence, and famous for that above all. After the 1940 invasion, the French language was '*verboten*'in Alsace. The streets were renamed, the milestones, the road-signs, even small notices, all had to be in German. One of the main nuclei of resistance was in the unlikely site of the Catholic Primary School, run by the Sisters of Divine Providence, in Ribeauvillé. From there came a constant stream of the spirit and language of France to maintain belief in that culture and confidence in ultimate release from bondage, in spite of the risk inherent in such anti-German activities.

The long and wayward main street works its way up between suspiciously trim traditional houses, including the *Pfifferhüs*, where the village band practised its craft, a fine black and white building with a pair of statues of the Annunciation, up as far as the Butchers' Tower, an ancient gateway dividing the upper from the lower towns. The upper part of the tower which carries a great clock, was set there in 1536 upon an earlier base. Below this tower, in the Place de l'Hôtel de Ville, is an attractive 16th century fountain.

Above the town the castle of St Ulrich is a good example of a fortified medieval family home. The duty of military sentinel was performed by the Haut-Ribeaupierre, rather higher up the mountainside. This was the original seat of the family of those powerful lords. They had, in course of time, become fat and plentiful, and by the twelfth century found their castle home over-crowded, as well, perhaps, as a bit primitive. St Ulrich was built to accommodate them, and, being relatively non-military, has managed to subsist until now with less damage than most of the others. This is well worth a visit, certainly by those who are *aficionados* of military architecture.

Southwards again along the road to Riquewihr, a short detour takes you up to another famous sight in this area, the fortified church of Hunawihr, which stands out over the vineyards it was intended to protect. The whole village has all the signs of a David determined to fight against any Goliath for its freedom and its wine. A bristling and stimulating place.

* * *

Ribeauvillé

Ribeauvillé – Pfiffertag

Riquewihr

A short drive further through the great vineyards brings you to Riquewihr, a magnificent medieval town that is even more famous for a magnificent Riesling, to which the inhabitants have, for centuries, devoted themselves. You can enjoy it to perfection at the *Auberge de Schöenenbourg*. History relates that in 1324, when the Counts of Horburg, lords of Riquewihr, in financial straits, sold their birthright to the Duke of Wurtemberg, the Prince-Bishop of Strasbourg, whose beady eye was fixed on the place, sent in troops to display his power and express his displeasure. The soldiery happily obliged, downing as much wine as they could, and did no damage in the town, even finding '*la chasse aux dames*' beyond their capabilities, and returned to Strasbourg not, however, too stupified to leave behind the great vats of wine stored in the place. Over the years other raids, often at the orders of the Duke of Lorraine, took place and were resisted by the *vignerons* of the town, sometimes successfully, sometimes not. What is clear about it all is that the attackers never harmed the goose of this golden egg: the vines were always left unharmed in these remarkably civilised forays.

Riquewihr is roughly rectangular in shape and is surrounded by ancient ramparts. Though some residents can take their cars into the narrow streets of the old town, visitors cannot. There are plenty of parking spaces round the outside of the walls. Inside, the streets are cobbled and are lined with a wonderful parade of ancient buildings, so many, in fact, that it is difficult to choose only a few to mention here.

At the top of the town the ramparts are pierced by the solid 16th century towers of the Obertor gate, in which the portcullis can still be seen, as well as the emplacement of the drawbridge. A second, thirteenth century gate stands a little further down the hill. This is the '*Dolder*'. Its stark military lines have been softened, in the course of time, and it has become residential. It has a curious appearance, tall, rather narrow, with windows, and a watch tower on the very top. Just in front of the Dolder is a fine Renaissance fountain of 1560, called the *Sinnbrunnen*.

Strike off to the left as you come down the hill through the arch of the Dolder, and you come to the ancient Jewish ghetto, whose low doors lead down steps to shops and wine shops, and here, in the Cour des Juifs, is the old prison, the Tower of Thieves, complete with torture chambers and dungeon. Alternatively, go off to the right, and you find the Kiener House of 1574, which has a contemporary bas-relief carving showing Death snatching away the Head of the Family. Opposite is the Stag Inn of about the same period.

You are, as it were, bombarded with splendid relics of the past as you go down the hill, or down the rue Latérale that runs parallel to the High Street. Almost every building catches the eye, especially, perhaps, the Preiss-Zimmer House which was an inn, the *Etoile*, and was built in 1686, a large place containing several interior yards. Lower down is the former Storks' Nest Inn, the oldest of all, now called Liebrich House (1535). This has a most picturesque yard with a rough wooden balcony above, the sort of place one imagines to have been used for the production of those lusty medieval farces, with the women in the balcony and the men standing on the rough cobbles, stones ready to hand if they were not kept amused, a farm-cart acting as stage. There is a gigantic wine-press there, and a well dating from 1603.

It is the total impression that makes Riquewihr one of the most attractive places to visit, in spite of the vast number of tourists there. Perhaps the lack of cars helps. Perhaps it is the fact that nothing looks doctored or false. Perhaps, even, it is the straightforward commercialism of the little bars offering a *dégustation* of the local

Kaysersberg – Main Square

wine. Or the wine itself. Who knows? What is clear, is that it imposes its antiquity and its simplicity without artifice, and that the whole atmosphere is somehow quite perfect.

So it is in Kaysersberg. On the way there, however, you pass through Kientzheim which deserves a mention. This is another old fortified village whose lower town gate, still standing, bears a carved head on it with its tongue stuck out to mock at any possible attackers. It is to be hoped that Kientzheim enjoyed success in the actual event. Outside the walls Kientzheim has the inscription: "*I love the past, good living and good wine*". A commendable philosophy! Inside the township is always gay with flowers, even flowing out of the ancient well, and the balconies of the aged houses are also colourfully decked out. It was in the vineyards here that the Tokay vines were first planted in Alsace.

Kaysersberg has my vote for the loveliest of the townships of Alsace. Its main street is hardly matched anywhere, and its culmination at the fortified Bridge with that beautiful view upsteam of its busy little river makes it unsurpassed and you can enjoy a superb meal at the Chambard in the Rue Général de Gaulle. The Renaissance front of the Town Hall, in a terra cotta so dark that it is almost burnt umber, hides an unsmartened little yard that has a neat and ancient balcony. At the side, by the Church, is a tiny churchyard with its own war cemetery and, under a rough shed roof, statues representing the Garden of Gethsemane scene. Somehow, unsophisticated, this is an appealing corner, watched over by the *donjon* of the old castle.

The church itself has a magnificent Romanesque doorway, with the usual sombre figures enlivened by creatures like pelicans and double-headed sirens. Inside are two magnificent works of art. Over the main altar there is a carved reredos that covers the last days of Christ in twelve panels which surround a central Crucifixion. The people represented, especially those around the Cross, are so malicious and malevolent, pictured with such horrid realism, that one is surprised, shocked perhaps, to see them there. This, in fact, was the style of German religious art, and this can be seen again at Colmar, especially among the works of Grunewald in the museum there. The artist responsible for the reredos at Kaysersberg also came from Colmar, one Jean Bongartz by name and he was clearly one of the same school as Grunewald. So was the creator of the panel, smaller and incomplete through later damage, over the altar of the chapel in the north aisle, a panel in polychrome and woodcarving of the Burial of Christ. Here the agony and sorrow are

Kaysersberg and Castle Ruins

superbly caught. Both works date from the early sixteenth century, which suggests that this was a specially prosperous period for Kaysersberg.

A little further on brings us to the small open space by the fortified bridge. The castle stands immediately above, as though still ready to rush soldiers down to the defence of the town. The bridge itself has a sort of rough crenellation and arrow-slits, and it has a small shrine in the middle. Towards the mountains the view is magical, a small weir set between a tall-pointed gingerbread house on the left, and a series of totally dissimilar houses on the right, houses of different heights, leaning outwards and sideways, propping each other up drunkenly, some low-browed and some supercilious. Weeping willows in front and shrub-covered hillside behind, and the mountains aloft in the distance. Glorious!

Across the bridge is the Brief House, all jutting gables and criss-crossed beams. Farther on, and no part of fairyland, is the house where Albert Schweitzer was born. It is a fine, equally early building, beautiful, but in a strange way more mundane.

Matters of fairyland are difficult to analyse. Kaysersberg, for me, is just that. Riquewihr belongs to real life. And yet, to a casual eye, they must look so much alike. So there it is. As the French are apt to say: *Chacun à son goût*!

It has a history, Kaysersberg has, real history. It was a Roman strongpoint, *Caesaris Mons* – Caesar's Mountain, fortified because it controlled a possible route over the mountains, via the Col du Bonhomme. Protected by the castle, it flourished in the Middle Ages. It was bought by the Emperor in the 13th century, developed walls, ramparts and town gates. Dukes of Lorraine raided it on occasion, and it held out against them. Here too the vineyards were sacrosanct. Under the Emperor it became a free town, enjoying Imperial protection and privileges. The castle was its safeguard, perched up on its '*motte*', of which the town was the bailey. A fine town and a strong town. Later, along with Kientzheim, it adopted the Tokay vine, and did well again.

This was not enough. During the last century this small *bourg* reached out into the future. Not wanting to be wholly dependent on the grape harvest, it invested in its other source of power, the swift-running waters of the river Weiss, and then, later still, utilised the coal deposits found and mined not far to the north; the textile industry was brought here, and paper was manufactured, both industries based on the natural raw materials of the locality. Progress has taken the paper trade to a more centralised and industrialised site by the river Rhine, and the textile making has been usurped by other centres. So Kaysersberg is back to its beginnings again. It is to be hoped it does not succumb entirely to cultivating the tourist.

Not far away, up in the mountains, Les Trois-Epis is truly the product of a fairy story. In 1491, so the story goes, there stood a statue of the Virgin Mary fixed to an oak tree. One Thierry Schoeré, a blacksmith, on his way to market, stopped there to say a prayer. The Virgin appeared, bathed in light, holding in her left hand an icicle, representing dire disaster if the district did not mend its ways, and in her right hand three ears of corn, (*trois épis*), standing for bumper harvests if it did. Thierry was commanded to go and preach this message in the market-place. Like other Old Testament prophets, he preferred silence. So the sack of corn he had bought became supernaturally heavy, immovable, and he was forced to speak of his vision. No laughter greeted his story. On the contrary the locals swore to improve their ways and Thierry went home with his corn. A chantry was built at the place where the heavenly visitor appeared. This is on a sandstone headland at over seven hundred metres, overlooking the plain, a singularly pleasant place that is still visited by pilgrims and has also become a popular holiday resort. The height of Le Galz is close by, a gentle hill walk for the energetic, and there are other good walks in the vicinity.

Down below, where the Fecht opens out into the plain, stands Turckheim, an ancient stronghold which, within the remains of its triangular fortifications has some good medieval and seventeenth century buildings. There were, and still are, at least, in part, three town gates, of which the lower, or Porte de France, is the most ancient, with a massive square tower that still supports a carefully preserved stork's nest. The Place Turenne has some large and imposing houses, some medieval and some of the seventeenth century. The Town Hall is basically a thirteenth century building, and the High Street contains some splendid Renaissance houses.

It was down from the mountains above the town that Turenne, Louis XIV's great general, after a long forced march across the mountains in winter, took the invading Imperial forces by surprise in 1674-5 and defeated them, although he was greatly outnumbered.

Further up the valley of the Fecht stands Munster. Apart from giving its name to the local hill cheese, a remarkably smelly but tasty one made by farmers in the high valleys, and an ornate Romanesque-style Protestant church, it has nothing much to commend it. Above, to the north, the mountains rise to a threatening peak. Here is to be found a battlefield of the First World War. Here gallant men laid down their lives, savaged each other for a square foot or two of land. The Germans held the summits of the Schratzmaennele and the Linge. In August, 1915, the French made their way up the west side and, in a bloody and desperate encounter managed to dispossess the enemy. Remnants of the German defences can still be seen at the summit. A little west of there at the Col de Wettstein there is a war cemetery containing the bodies of 3000 French troops who died in this action. From there the N.417 leads to one of the main crossroads of the highlands of the Vosges, the Col de la Schlucht, which is touched on in a later chapter.

Although the Route des Vins continues on its way south, we are leaving it here, since the main growing area is done. More vineyards, of course, are found right down to the far end of the mountains, as well as many attractive villages, so we must go down to see them.

11. Colmar

Colmar is a large town with very considerable suburban development. It has never ceased to grow, and diversify its activities since the early Middle Ages, by which time it was already a wealthy and independent centre. In the fifteenth and sixteenth centuries it reached such a zenith of commercial success that it also became an artistic centre of importance. It is the result of this that makes it today such a lure for visitors who come from all over the world.

The streets of the medieval town are almost perfect, all the splendour of the true Alsatian style massed in one small nucleus. It is only by a hair's breadth that it manages to avoid looking artificial, a stage set for some Ruritanian extravaganza. What saves it is its obvious authenticity: the '*Pfister* house', for example, is so outrageously theatrical that it must be genuine, as, really, is the '*Schongauer*' house on the other corner of this cross-street. Stage sets for romantic plays are usually, inevitably, all the clichés strung together. It is this unexpectedness that makes Colmar a delight to see, even though you may have to elbow your way through hordes of tourists to have a front-row view of any of the fine buildings and artistic treasures of the place.

Colmar grew up as a free town even before the great days of the Holy Roman Empire. It successfully defended itself during the darkest of the Dark Ages, supported by Charlemagne who made it an Imperial residence. Under his aegis it increased in strength and wealth, and its unity and combined search for peaceful progress that

Colmar – Balcony of Town Guard's Headquarters

Colmar – Petite Venise

turned it into a city of doves, with a communal dovecote in the middle of it. So the name *Villa Columbaria* led by the wearing process of time and the laziness of men's tongues to Colmar.

Commercial success came from its position astride the north-south all-weather trading route, the '*Bergstrasse*'' running along the plain, and on the confluence of the Fecht and the Lauch, both of which led up to possible crossing-points in the mountains. Wealth, here again, bred jealousy among neighbouring rivals. Commercial in-fighting at that time was less sophisticated, doubtless, but no less ruthless than that of today; take-overs happened not by financial jugglery but by main force. And the Church Militant had its finger well in the centre of the pie along with the Dukes and other men of power and rank. Let the story of Roesselmann and the Prince-Bishop of Strasbourg (history is quite clear that this is not the same Prince-Bishop as the villain of the Riquewihr story) spotlight this period of commercial free-for-all.

Roesselmann was Mayor of Colmar, and, in that independent and commerce-orientated place, a commoner, an artisan, the offspring of a tanner, a social distinction he shared, it may be recalled, with the mother of William the Conqueror. Whether out of snobbery or sheer greed, the Bishop persuaded the local aristocracy, mostly only recently elevated scions of the strong rogues who had carved out their authority and castles in the mountains by preying on peaceful traders to join him in an attack on this prosperous plum. To make sure of success, the Bishop played a trump card; he excommunicated Roesselmann, who fled and found refuge at the court of Rudolph of Hapsburg.

A little later on, Roesselmann returned to Colmar, now held by the Bishop and his friends, hidden in a wine-barrel. His supporters, at this signal, rose and turned on the conquerors, and Rudolph's troops arrived at the psychological moment to rout the invaders. Naturally the Prince of the Church was not going to take this lying down; a squadron of his men, disguised in the colours of Rudolph of Hapsburg, later entered the town. They were unmasked and driven out, but, alas, Roesselmann, at the head of the town militia, was killed in the process. Dangerous, but somehow simpler, days, those of the Middle Ages.

During the prosperous years, from the late fourteenth century to the end of the sixteenth, Colmar created its own mini-Renaissance, a local affair with a strongly Alsatian flavour, and gave birth or a home to a number of remarkable artists. That golden century also saw the building of that superlative collection of houses that make up the present centre (still the administrative centre) of the town, not only houses and shops, but religious and official structures of all kinds. Among the best known of these are the Convent of Unterlinden, now a municipal museum with some splendid exhibits, the Parish Church of St Martin, the old Franciscan Church of St Matthew, now a Protestant church, the ancient headquarters of the Town Guard with its Renaissance porch and balcony, the Customs House, and so on; the list is endless.

In view of the activities of the ambitious prelates of Strasbourg, the reforms of Luther and the preaching of Calvin may well have been necessary, but the horrors then imposed on the world by religious fanaticism make those activities seem mere peccadillos. As elsewhere, the rise of Protestantism and the ensuing hatred immersed Colmar and sucked away its peacefulness and wealth. Religious war was followed by political fratricide, and the citizens, having little political bias of their own, found themselves facing attack from all sides. In desperation they sought the shield of France and were soon merged into the French state. This worked successfully for them; Colmar became an administrative and judicial centre for the province. One or two stalwart, four-square classical buildings, the old Hospital, the Palace of the Council, the Town Hall, bear witness to the staid, respectable, establishment Colmar of the eighteenth century.

Today Colmar is an active, aggressive complex of industrial and agricultural activity with considerable expansion on all sides of the ancient centre, and it has found the means to continue the shrewd and independent business expertise that led to that first flowering of the town. The whole area around is dominated by Colmar, vineyards especially, but also farming, hop-fields, sweet corn, cabbages, factories, the new port construction at Neuf-Brisach, all these operate in the shadow of Colmar and have their mainspring in Colmar. The population has doubled since 1900, and now stands at over 70,000 inhabitants. The nearby villages have all swollen in size to accommodate the big commuter population. Even the Fecht valley up as far as Munster and beyond is full now of the houses of the prosperous executives.

* * *

The best way to look at the old town is to wander at leisure and without an ordered itinerary. You are bound to see everything you should see; it's all so close together. If you leave your car in the vast car park of the Place Rapp (a sort of magnet for vehicles), you will probably walk off towards St Martin's Church. You will see the simple old Guard House, its only piece of pretentiousness the fine Renaissance balcony from which the town officials spoke their oath of office and important news was announced.

Across the way is the Parish Church, often called the Cathedral, largely of the late thirteenth century, smallish, intimate, with massive pillars, some fine early windows, and a magnificent sculpted Crucifixion behind the main altar. The famous painting, the 'Virgin of the Rose Trees', by Schongauer, which used to be on view here, has recently been removed to the Dominican Church, not far away, where a charge is levied to view it. The picture dates from 1473 and it is a very beautiful, if somewhat sentimental representation of Mary and Child in almost scarlet robes, against a gold background trellised with red roses and green leafage, the whole in a sculptured arched frame with intertwined fronds and angels playing instruments. It really is very beautiful.

Coming back from the 'Cathedral' you come to a crossroads and,

Colmar – Krutenau District

Unterlinden Museum in Colmar

as striking as anything else here, the '*Pfister*' house, with a lot of brown woodwork, an overhanging gallery or mirador, an odd turret at the corner, and various saintly paintings running along the wall below the gallery. It was built in 1537 by a wealthy hatter from Besançon. It is now an antique dealer's shop. Across the street is the beautiful façade of the Swan House, the painter Schongauer's house, and immediately beyond, the house of another painter, Isenmann. All these houses, of the sixteenth century, show the height of splendour and artistic interest that existed in Colmar in that century.

And not far away, rightly, is the symbol of the economic power that created this artistic outburst – the Customs House, the Koïfus, a good honest piece of building from the late fifteenth century. The ground floor acted as warehouse for goods subject to local duty, and the upper storey was the meeting room and court-house of the magistrates. The whole building, unadorned, solid, powerful, is exactly right, a splendid example of straightforward, no-nonsense self-confidence, the hallmark of the great days of the town. Its abiding beauty, and it *is* beautiful, lies in its unpretentiousness; it has a wooden balcony, plain and unsculptured, though massed with flowers in season, under the tall, curving pitched roof with the typical patterns of tiles in a discreet design of diamonds, in equally discreet colouring. A little spiral staircase squats in a hexagonal tower at one corner under an ogee-shaped hat. The whole is supported on a range of great, flattened arches resting on efficient, undecorated, rectangular pillars. It is a notable piece of building, hardly architecture perhaps since it seems just to have 'growed', and not all at once, but it is essentially satisfying.

There is still much more to see. A few steps beyond the Customs House runs the thread of the river Lauch where the old markets, the fruit market and the fish market, occupied the small open spaces, and where the traders had their houses. All along the sides of the little river are the ancient houses, hiding behind willows or peeping out from behind their creepers. There is a local school there with the children studying, playing in the ancient playground, or rushing off home on bike or moped. Colmar, like Strasbourg, is a place of youth. This area is called, unimaginatively, *Petite Venise*, part of which is the Krutenau Quarter. It has splendidly picturesque corners, with fountains, and buildings glimpsed from tiny bridges.

The fact that so much of Colmar was preserved from the customary German fury when they were on the run in 1944/5 was the result

Colmar

of some notable American-French co-operation. The Germans were holding out in a pocket round Colmar. General de Lattre de Tassigny was in charge of the operation to dislodge them. Under his command were several American divisions, and, in the pincer movement that was the main part of the Allied strategy, one of these, the 109th Regiment of Infantry, was first to reach the edge of the town. The American commander, General Milburn, ordered his regiment to halt there to allow General Schlesser and his French tanks to enter the town first. Here the French *élan* paid off; the troops seized Colmar, without any artillery preparation, by the suddenness of their attack, and almost no damage was done to the old buildings.

Among these is one so far almost without a mention but which must be visited by anyone interested in medieval, or indeed Western European, art, the ancient Convent of Unterlinden, basically a thirteenth century building which now houses a superb museum. The housing of the Art collection is itself a noble and restrained building, but it is what it contains, the magnificent reredos or retable of the Issenheim Altar, along with other fine primitive paintings, that makes its real glory.

This great and strange work of art dates from 1500, when the Prior of the House of the Antonites at Issenheim prevailed on Mathias Grünewald of Colmar to adorn his chapel. With the aid of his pupils, this the artist did, and did magnificently. The work on display at the museum consists of a central part, on one side, consisting of a high-relief polychrome and gilt wooden representation of St Anthony between Saints Jerome and Augustine. All the figures have faces of such realism and character that they hardly seem a medieval work. The other side has a superb Crucifixion of terrible realism, the agony so clear, with the Mother Mary in white and so distraught, supported by John, and Mary Magdalene on her knees with her gold hair hanging low about her.

About these two central panels are other, smaller paintings, all marked by the accuracy of the observation and the representation of feelings, the Annunciation, the Nativity and the concert of Angels, the Entombment and the Resurrection, the Temptations of St Anthony with creatures worthy of the imagination of Hieronymus Bosch. Though there is glory in these paintings, there is much horror, a foresight perhaps of the dreadful years yet to come when the new heresies tore the world apart. The same horrors, the evil of men face to face with Christ, the puzzlement, doubt and sarcasm of the elders listening to the young Christ as he interpreted the scriptures in the temple, the agony of the Crucified Man, can be seen in another series of panels of an altar-piece by that other great Colmar artist, Schongauer. These are shown in the same room in the museum, and date from a few years earlier. These scenes, too, are quite staggering in the impact they produce. You cannot, must not, miss these overwhelming works of art.

Colmar is a place of great beauty, a town of flowers, of tall high-pitched roofs done in patterns of coloured and varnished tiles, shining and fresh, of leaning house-fronts and carved beams, of narrow streets and exciting glimpses of a balcony or a painted facade. That is the centre of the old town. Not far away, near the station, in the Rue de la République, is a modest and pleasant little hotel that we have liked, *La Chaumière*.

The outskirts of the town are quite different, modern suburban houses, concrete high-rise blocks, factories, the new housing developments, superior, executive-type urbanisations. Old villages have been sucked into the maw, buses bring schoolchildren in from wide areas. Out on the Strasbourg road, there is a very large recreational complex with a fine open-air theatre. That is just short of Ostheim, a village much damaged in the 1944/5 fighting. This is commemorated by the unusual war memorial, the single end of the old parish church topped by a stork's nest, again most carefully preserved.

Between Colmar and the Rhine there is still a good deal of cultivation, rather more early vegetables than general agriculture. The persistence of this has somewhat halted the building development on that side, until you come to Neuf-Brisach. This is one of the first places to be fortified by Vauban after the cession to France of various cities and strongholds after the Thirty Years War. It was not just a strengthening of existing medieval walls, but a total redesigning of the town. Set within the octagonal fortifications of Vauban's usual style, the town is constructed in blocks of buildings divided from each other by exactly similar streets set at right angles. All very logical and formal, and completely foreign to the haphazard lack of planning in the traditional Alsatian villages. Breisach, across the river, on the German side, with its old castle above it, looks much more picturesque. However, Neuf-Brisach did suffer severely during the black winter of 1944/5.

Down by the Rhine bridge here, there is one of the giant canal locks and power stations, that of Vogelgrün, that have already been described. It is here, too, that some of Colmar's industries have been sited, alongside the canal where wharves have been established to handle Colmar's own traffic. This has added to the speed and efficiency of all the operations. Now far downstream from there we have, with enjoyment, watched what was described as an 'International Fishing Competition', at which a great army of anglers was massed round what looked like a very muddy little pond. It is of course, not difficult to hold an international meeting so close to a national frontier.

12. La Route des Crêtes and Mulhouse

It is time now to leave Colmar across the main traffic arteries of the valley and the plain, and to climb back once more into the mountains. The roads are good and the hills not too steep, and even an underpowered Fiat finds them well within its capabilities.

The impression of sheer height, or even sheer bulk, depends on the surroundings. A single lofty peak set in a plain, looks arresting and vast by contrast with the ground level of the plain. One or two peaks of the Vosges are striking because they stand out from the lower hills around them. Thus the pointed Schratzmaennele, by Hohrodberg, above Munster, is a more eye-catching mountain than the higher Hohneck which is lost in the surrounding heights that seem to lift it up.

This is where the majestic *Route des Crêtes* now runs. For most of the length of the High Vosges this strategic road, build by military engineers after 1918, keeps along the line of the topmost points. Most of the time the road goes through massed pine forests mixed with beeches and a few other species, and so it offers little sense of height, except, perhaps, in winter, until there is some tremendous shaft that opens out downwards, as, for instance, at the Gazon du Faing, where a bold crag offers an impressive view.

Perhaps the top of the Hohneck gives the best overall effect of height. From it you look outwards over a tremendous vista of rounded peaks sleeping up there above the Alsatian plain below. It has the advantage, too, that it can be reached without too much

Col de la Schlucht

effort. But even from there these great heights look rather like bears, snoozing contentedly up there in the sky.

Most of the best viewpoints require some walking to reach them, as also do the various lakes that are to be found near the *Route*, or within the distance of a short detour. The Lac Blanc and the Lac Noir can, in fact, be reached by car by turning off the *Route des Crêtes* not long after heading south from the Col du Bonhomme on to the D.48. These two lakes, of which the former is 300 feet higher than the latter, are linked by underground pipes. That way the water that has flowed down to the Lac Noir by day is pumped up again at night, when power demands are slight, to the Lac Blanc. Then, as it runs down again during the day it works turbines that make the power for the high demand periods. Both these lakes are picturesque, the Lac Blanc larger and dominated by a fortress-like crag, the Lac Noir surrounded by granite cliffs that give it its dark and grim appearance.

Beyond the Col de la Schlucht, where the N.417 crosses the mountains to link Gérardmer with Colmar, the road climbs round the shoulder of the Hohneck and a steep little road snakes its way up to the mountain's peak. This is a breathtaking view on a clear day; you dominate Germany from there, and the Alps seem only a stone's throw away!

Probably the most dramatic section of the *Route* is that round Le Markstein. Here the road, with typical French engineering efficiency, runs along crests, by precipices, under overhangs, and showers the driven with splendid and extensive views. The driver, you hope, will be concentrating on the road!

Under the eastern slopes of the Grand Ballon, at just over 1500 metres, up which you can climb on a path by the hotel, you will have the opportunity again, if the weather is kind, to marvel at the gigantic spaces opened up along the bare shoulders of the mountain. Up here, as elsewhere along the way, you are above the tree-line, a skiers' playground in winter and a fine grazing area for farm stock in high summer, when the snow-covered land becomes coated in a springy turf, ideal for walking.

From here, once past the National War Memorial at Vieil Armand, that peak further to the east which looks down steeply on the plain and was a prize bitterly and wastefully fought for, especially in 1915, the road swoops and swirls down to the lowlands at Uffholtz. There are some grand snatches of view out over the Rhine to the Black Forest as the trees open out and sudden tight corners permit.

* * *

From there it is a short step to Thann, another creation of some religious tale. It is surprising in this cynical age how many places in Europe, seem to have been the repository of some sacred vestige of a saint's humanity. Here it was the thumb of St Thiebaut, Bishop of Gubbio in Umbria. Every circumstance seems to be against the story, and yet it all gained great credence in the twelfth century. Supported by the Lord of Engelbourg a chapel was erected to accommodate the thumb. The chapel became a monastic house, and the abbey grew and grew in power and wealth. The church is a quite magnificent late-Gothic building, beautiful and ornate, with some remarkable fifteenth century stalls. These were carved by a master's hand, a man with an impish sense of humour; there are comic and fabulous beasts and people done in wicked comparison. The great

Mulhouse – Husslin Zur Sunnen

west door, too, is an architectural masterpiece, very large, very tall and magnificently carved, with scenes from the life of the Virgin Mary in the middle, the Adoration of the Magi on one side, and the Crucifixion on the other.

The old town was severely damaged, in the winter of 1944-5 when, for some seven weeks, the opposing forces faced each other and slogged it out here. This is especially sad since old accounts describe Thann as one of the finest examples of Alsatian architecture.

* * *

Back on the *Route*, the road passes the pathway up to the Gazon du Faing with a climb up to another splendid vantage point. A bit further on, where other cars are likely to be already parked, a path leads eastwards from the 5 km stone to a point overlooking the Lac Vert whose greenness is caused, so one reads, by lichens.

Mulhouse, twelve or so miles away is a very wealthy and very powerful industrial city, so wealthy and powerful indeed that it has no time to be even moderately polite to unwealthy visitors.

Parts of Mulhouse are very attractive, even though most of the city is modern. There is the Place de la Réunion, so called because it commemorates the final union of this free city with France, during the Revolutionary regime, in 1798. The Place is surrounded, on two sides, at least, by 16th and 17th century houses and shops, tall and narrow, again, and forming a compact and coherent union to each side of the beautiful Husslin zur Sunnen, of 1418, with its curved projecting frontage and wall-paintings. Just round the corner, too, is the William Tell Inn with carved timbers, a balcony and window-boxes.

The eastern side of the square is filled by the Town Hall, a strange and striking piece of architecture, built in 1552 by one Backstorfter, as is recorded, along with the names of later restorers, on the side of it. It is a two-storey, provincial Renaissance building of simple design, painted in terra-cotta and with pictures, done by highlighting and shading the basic colour, of the Virtues and of Biblical scenes. There is a covered ceremonial staircase at the front, with a double set of stairs. At the side of the Hall hangs a heavy stone mask, the *Klapperstein* or Slanderers' stone. Evil-tongued gossips were condemned to carry this, hanging round their neck, through the town, as their punishment. It is an appealing facet of this

Mulhouse Town Hall

hard-faced, go-getting, industrial society that the old Town Hall, quaint and unsophisticated, still stands.

The church on the north side, which dominates the square, is of the Protestant faith, and is a reconstruction of an earlier 'temple' (as the French call Protestant churches), built in the Gothic style in 1858. It contains the fourteenth century stained glass windows of the former building. It may, at first, seem strange that the main place of worship here should be a Protestant church, but down in this southern corner of Alsace we are not so far from the centre of Calvinism at Geneva. Mulhouse, indeed, had reason to be especially influenced. In 1466 Mulhouse became disenchanted with the combination of Alsatian towns and cities, called the *Decapolis*, to which it belonged, since it found that this union was insufficiently strong to offer reasonable protection to its members. The inhabitants considered that links with the Swiss would be more of a protection against the depredations of greedy Alsatian nobles. They formed a union with Basle, Berne and Soleure as a start. Later, in 1515, a full scale treaty of alliance was signed with all thirteen cantons of the Swiss Confederation. The independence that this gave Mulhouse lasted, in fact, until 1798, since Mulhouse had been omitted from the provisions of the Treaty of Westphalia in 1648, which handed Alsace over to France.

Not far away from the Place de la Réunion, almost at the end of the Rue de Metz, is an interesting contrast of structures. At the far end is the Tower of Europe, a soaring modern block, 30 storeys high, with triangular, concave sides, all glass and concrete, set in the Place de l'Europe, a pedestrian precinct with the ancient European city coats of arms in marble mosaic underfoot. Near the bottom end is the only remnant of the ancient city walls, two high pointed arches and a small guard port, rather sad and forlorn there, outside the Lycée and the terrifying current of cars that pours round it. It is called the Tower of Bollwerk.

You cannot go far in Mulhouse without running into some aspect of its industrial strength, both of the earlier basis of its wealth and of more recent developments. The past is enshrined in a rather pleasant square set round a shrubby garden and called Place de la Bourse. This dates from around 1832 and is made up of some strangely evocative arcaded buildings in terra-cotta and off-white which somehow manage to suggest some decaying Lombardy town.

In 1746 three men created the *Société d'Industrie* at Mulhouse by inventing and developing a process of printing on materials. A textile industry already existed both in, and all around Mulhouse, so that the cloth was readily available. These three men, headed by J.J. Dollfus, launched on the world the printed cloth, known universally as 'Indian'. Because of this, and by carefully safeguarding the secrets of the manufacturing process, in spite, doubtless, of every attempt at industrial espionage, the city of Mulhouse grew and grew; the population rose, between the end of the eighteenth and the end of the nineteenth centuries, from 6,000 to 100,000 inhabitants. The new industrialists were leaders in the field of social welfare, and the workers were housed in fine new estates round the perimeter of the city, each in a semi-detached house with its own garden.

That golden age ceased in 1871 with the Prussian occupation. The masters of the textile firms withdrew to other parts of France, and they carried away their secrets. This brought about a serious crisis, among the employees. Only the discovery and development of great potassium beds just to the north of the city made industrial progress possible. Even then, and after the 1914-18 War, when financial investment remained shy of this border region, industrial stability remained foreign to this area.

It was not until 1954 that a new forward impetus came. Then it was created by renewed confidence following the Franco-German *rapprochement*, by a remodelling of textile methods, and by an influx, government sponsored, of new industries, mainly mechanical and chemical. At present, as elsewhere in the region, there is some recession, but the outlook is considered to be fair for this corner of France.

In November, 1944, French troops advanced rapidly through the Belfort gap and thence, by a southward detour, reached Mulhouse on the 21st. There was little opposition here, and the city was recaptured without difficulty. Further north the Germans held out and later, helped by the flooding of the river Ill established a strong pocket round Colmar. At the southern edge of this were Ensisheim and Guebwiller.

Ensisheim, one of the principal stopping-points on the medieval *Bergstrasse*, was a wealthy and artistic town with much good architecture. Bombardments during the winter campaign of 1944/5 took heavy toll of the place, and it is now rather a sad relic of those palmy fifteenth and sixteenth century days that is to be seen in the splendid Hôtel de la Gouronne and the early 16th century Town Hall, well restored and a good example of its period.

Guebwiller has been left with a good church of the transition period between Romanesque and Gothic, a good late Gothic Town

Mulhouse – Bollwerk Tower and European Tower

Mulhouse

Hall, a glorious valley that bears its name, and a striking feminist legend that includes an object lesson in the dangers of allowing the clergy to become too powerful.

The story begins away back in the Dark Ages some way up the Guebwiller valley that heads straight for the Grand Ballon. There, at Murbach, a Religious House was founded, it is said, by St Pirmin, in 727. Like other monastic foundations it was adopted by the local lord, Count Eberhard of Eguisheim, another of the ubiquitous descendents of the prolific Duke Etichon. This was powerful enough protection, but better was to follow; Charlemagne himself lent his support. The result was that Murbach became an aristocratic establishment. It prospered enormously, became very wealthy indeed, and tyrannised the locality. Part of its huge late Romanesque abbey Church can still be seen.

The Abbot was, *ex-officio*, a Prince of the Holy Roman Empire and the Brothers were all Knights. The story comes now to Guebwiller, where the townsfolk, to protect themselves from the rapacious brethren, built a wall round their little town. Whether it succeeded in its original intention is not related, but the wall was still standing in the fifteenth century during a civil war, one of the last internal convulsions after the Hundred Years War and before the central authority became established. It hardly matters where Guebwiller stood in the matter. It was under attack one February night in 1445, and the enemy managed to cross the defensive ditches on the ice. Only one woman appears to have been awake. She was Brigitte Schick, and, seeing the arrival of the attackers outside the walls, she lit the alarm signal and rushed about, shrieking so loudly, or so terrifyingly, that the enemy withdrew in disorder, leaving their scaling-ladders behind, bearing witness to the power of the female voice raised in anger.

But there is further evidence of that power enshrined in another village not far away. At Rouffach is an even better story and one reminiscent of, if not the inspiration for, a well known classic of the Spanish Theatre, *Fuenteovejuna*, by Lope de Vega. In 1106, the Emperor, who had a castle here at Rouffach, became enamoured of a local girl. Imagining, one supposes, that any girl would be flattered by the attentions of her liege lord, he had her kidnapped one Easter Sunday. The women of Rouffach, roused by such wickedness and working on their husbands, led an attack in force on the castle. The Emperor and his men, appalled by the sight of these wild women, fled, leaving behind crown, sceptre and Imperial robe.

* * *

It was at Rouffach, in February, 1945, that the Americans coming from the north met the French Moroccan mountain division who had come up from the south, thus cutting across the Colmar pocket and driving the Germans back across the Rhine

The town is a pleasant place with a good early Gothic church, and a picturesque Place de la République that contains a remarkably fine Corn Exchange building with an imposing balcony served by double staircases outside the front that faces the square, a front that rises to a fine stepped gable-end. Just behind this is the neat Witches' Tower, square, balustraded at the top, and with a tall four-sided hat surmounted by one of those permanent nostalgic stork's nests. It would be a neat sequel to the story of the women if this were a tower of the original castle of the Emperor.

Nearer to Colmar the village of Eguisheim deserves a mention, if only because it seems to appear as a sort of refrain in these pages. This is not, however, the only reason. Too far from the 1944/5 battle lines, it has been lucky enough, to remain almost as it was in the 16th century. It is an excellent example of basic medieval planning, the houses ranged in circles within the town walls that encircle the protecting flanks of the castle. The castle itself has disappeared and the church is modern, though it contains elements of the previous building, but the houses display a splendid procession of all types of dwellings, from the lavish houses of the wealthy to the humble, narrow, projecting, balconied, window-boxed, shuttered abodes of the poor. And all drawn up, like sheep in their pen, not quite ordered or dragooned but fitting in as best they can, protected against the harsh wolves outside.

On the hill above the town are the three massive towers, a landmark over a wide area, of the ancient castle built by Eberhard d'Eguisheim, in the eighth century. This part of the record seems improbable; stone-built castles of that age are few and far between. Perhaps the towers came later. It must have been an enormous structure in any case; these remnants are very well separated. Eberhard, the builder, was Saint Odile's nephew, and the family pop up all over the province.

* * *

The Alsatian dialect is heard everywhere, but the Lorraine dialect I have never heard.

This minor difference between the Alsatians and Lorrainers may, in fact, mark something more fundamental, the drive and self-sufficiency of the former and the greater acceptance, of the latter. That's not really fair to Lorraine. Alsace has always been in the centre of European affairs, of European trade, owing to the proximity of the Rhine and the great north-south all-weather road along the foothills. Lorraine is cut off from all this by the Vosges, and its outlook is bound to be towards France. It is only in the north, the black and yellow north, that Lorraine has links with an outside world other than France.

Alsace is better placed, even if it is because money is coming in from across the nearby frontiers. The German miracle has spilled over into this part of the Rhineland. Co-operation is the order of the day. Alsace will inevitably benefit from Franco-German competition to utilise its resources. The province, too, is outward-looking and must profit from the Common Market, to which, through Strasbourg, it is closely associated.

From the point of view of the tourist trade, it is the Vosges that will develop most strongly, not so much as a ski resort – their slopes can never be exciting enough for expert skiers – but as a holiday centre. At present they are, almost everywhere, peaceful, quiet, tranquil. It is possible to go to a farmhouse and enjoy a country meal of bread and the home-made '*munster*' or a sausage. This is a very special, very old-world feature. But as the camp-sites, the lakeside developments, the urban entertainments spread and grow, that essential peace, too, must go.

So the message is clearly written on the wall: Go at once to this land, or this uneasy partnership of lands. Go while there is still time. This is where fairyland is to be found, and the romantic Middle Ages, raise a head that is still bloody but, as yet, unbowed.

Postscript

The wise traveller in France obeys three rules. He travels on minor roads, he eats from the Red Michelin Guide, and he stays in *Logis de France* hotels. Many people now camp, and France has many excellent campsites for the roving traveller. A more settled holiday can be arranged by hiring a gîte or a country cottage. A list of guides or information on these various choices is given in the bibliography. Full information on the provinces of Alsace and Lorraine can be obtained by writing to The French Government Tourist Office, 178 Piccadilly, London W1.

The following hotels or restaurants are worth visiting when in the area, and all offer a *menu touristique* as well as *à la carte*.

Altkirch (Haut-Rhin)	*Auberge Sundgovienne*
Ammerschwihr (Haut-Rhin)	*Aux Armes de France*
Artzenheim (Haut-Rhin)	*Auberge d'Artzenheim*
Bar-le-Duc (Meuse)	*Metz et Commerce*
Belleville (Meurthe et Meuse)	*Le Bistroquet*
Colmar (Haut-Rhin)	*Au Fer Rouge*
Epinal (Vosges)	*Les Ducs de Lorraine*
Gérardmer (Vosges)	*Au Grand Cerf*
Kaysersberg (Haut-Rhin)	*Chambard*
Liverdun (Meurthe-et-Moselle)	*Hôstellerie de la Gare*
Marlenheim (Bas Rhin)	*Hôstellerie du Cerf*
Metz (Moselle)	*La Maison des Têtes*

Mulhouse (Haut-Rhin)	*La Buchèrie*
Mulhouse (Haut-Rhin)	*La Poste (at Predisheim)*
Neiderhaslach (Bas Rhin)	*La Pomme d'Or*
Ribeauvillé (Haut-Rhin)	*Clôs St Vincent*
Rouffach (Haut-Rhin)	*Château D'Isembourg*
Strasbourg (Bas-Rhin)	*Bruesehiesel*
	La Chaumière
	La Châteaubriand
	Au Pont St Martin

FOOD

Both Alsace and Lorraine are still primarily agricultural areas. Their traditional cuisine, therefore, must be expected to reflect this. There is, however, some difference between the two; Lorraine, the wetter, being on the windward side of the mountains, is almost wholly a dairy region, and Alsace, with a drier climate and a fine alluvial soil, devotes itself more to crop-raising. In both areas the pig is the main animal reared for meat, and pork and bacon are plentiful.

It is little wonder, in view of this, that the *Quiche* is the only dish to bear the name of Lorraine. This is one of the supreme creations of the pastry-cook, and that is a trade that has always been respected here. Eggs, cream, bacon and herbs baked in a fine short crust make a delicious meal. Another typical savoury dish of the region is the '*potée*' (difficult for an Anglo-Saxon to order without a smile!), the regional variation, using bacon instead of beef, of the '*pot-au-feu*', a rich casserole in which the local white cabbage plays a useful part.

But Lorraine's cuisine seems mostly to turn to desserts and confectionery, open fruit tarts, like sweet quiches, sponge cakes, the special macaroons '*des Soeurs*' of Nancy, sugary ramekins, honey cakes and sugar almonds. Just another outward sign of Lorraine's romantic spirit? Here again, however, there is a more down to earth side to it – these things do not come too cheap to the unwary purchaser!

Alsace, as you might expect, is more serious about its food, and the inhabitants are little given to dieting or anxiety about cholesterol levels. Their gastronomic tastes are similar to those of their neighbours across the Rhine, plenty of meat dishes, of sausage and other wurst, of *pâtés* and *terrines*. Michelin tells us that there exist 42 different local *pâtés*, of which, of course, the Strasbourg *pâté de foie gras*, made there for centuries, rich, smooth and succulent, is the supreme monarch. Amongst the meat dishes, you will be amazed at the variety of ways the pig can be served. And all quite delicious!

Probably the most frequently eaten dish in Alsace (and you find it often beyond the mountains as well) is *choucroute* (or *sauerkraut*). The production of this is big business, as has already been pointed out, and canned *choucroute* saves many a housewife's bacon. But here and there it is still pickled in the traditional way. The dried white cabbage leaves are packed in coarse salt in barrels, layer upon layer, covered in water and under a weighted lid. There it stands for several weeks, the scum skimmed off as it forms, and then the resulting compressed and marinaded cabbage is cooked, as it is required, with local white white, and is served with pieces of pork and bacon and perhaps a sausage or two and boiled potatoes. It makes a remarkably filling and satisfying dish, washed down with wine or beer, and, if funds are running low, it is a very economical one.

As well as pork and bacon, fish is popular on the Alsatian table. This means fresh water fish from Rhine and Ill and mountain streams. The fish farmers of the northern hills are not there so much to supply the basic commodity for sportsmen's entertainment but to provide, in due course, for the tables of Strasbourg and the other cities and towns. So trout, pike, perch, carp, salmon, even eels, appear, prepared usually with wine and/or cream to tempt the trenchermen of Alsace or from overseas.

If that is not enough, there is also a wide variety of poultry, not simply the poor little factory-farmed and tasteless chickens, but real, strutting capons, geese, fat ducklings, rich in flavour and always helped along by wine.

And to follow? A cream-filled apple tart? A slice of cherry flan thick with whipped cream? A piece of traditional, fattening Kugelhof, a sort of lardy cake with raisins, sultanas and almonds?

Or cheese? As well as being well stocked with all the usual range of cheeses, Alsace and Lorraine both have their own, a potent cream cheese called *Munster* on the eastern slopes of the Vosges and *Géromé* on the western. They are the product of the mountains, made by traditional methods in the farmsteads up by the summer high pastures, the Chaumes, that spring to life when the snows depart. It is pleasant in summer to visit these highland farms and to enjoy a rustic snack there of home-made bread, butter, brawn perhaps (*Kalerei*), and *Munster*.

If you prefer to take your own picnic, there is plenty of variety to be had from the delicatessen or the food store. With a long French loaf, a selection of *pâtés*, cheese, and a bottle or so of Sylvaner or Chasselas wine, you will have a feast.

Take some *munster* with you by all means, but don't attempt to bring any back for another day. Munster has one of the most powerful pongs in the world, a smell that creeps and burrows and clings; it pervades the car, the hotel room, the caravan; it lays siege and saps the foundations; it embraces everything and stays with it; it never lets go! So keep it for the open air.

DRINK

Since 1918 the Alsatian wine industry has slowly and successfully been restored and rehabilitated by patient devotion of the growers. Most of the product is white, and it ranges from the splendid Rieslings and Traminers that fetch good prices in the world markets, to the unpretentious but very palatable Sylvaners and Chasselas.

Several different types of grape are used to produce these wines. Among others that appear in only small quantities are the Pinot Gris, or Alsatian Tokay, which was originally brought from Hungary, and the Pinot Blanc which gives a white wine described as 'comfortable, solid, perfectly balanced, but without any special character'. The four main types, though, are the Riesling, described by the same expert as 'one of the most noble of white grapes, producing elegant, fruity wine', the Traminer, spicy and seductive (the Don Juan of wines!), the Sylvaner, lighter and refreshing, and the Chasselas, which gives the bulk of the *vins ordinaires* of the region.

There are others, perhaps more for the palate of the pundits, but those mentioned should satisfy most people. It is best to go to Riquewihr or Ribeauvillé or to one of the other halting-points on the *Route des Vins* and set about tasting seriously, letting someone else worry about the driving. Then you can decide for yourself. In any case, the adjectives used by wine-scribes never seem to convey the reality of flavour, scent and sparkle that you get from a taste of the magic liquid. Best of all is a glass or two (or so!) on a sun-warmed pasture up in the mountains with a crunchy loaf of bread and a tasty cheese.

Alongside the wines are distilled a fine array of liqueurs using the fruits of this rich soil: Kirsch des Vosges (cherry), Quetsche (plum), Mirabelle (another plum), Framboise (raspberry), and a Marc derived from the Traminer grape.

Another great speciality of Alsace and of Northern Lorraine, and a boon to the thirsty wayfarer, is beer. Hops and barley are grown in great quantities for this essential to good living, and the insatiable Alsatians consume impressive amounts.

Every race and every district has its own built-in certainties about what beer must be like. Alsatian and Lorrainer beers may not match up to a real English bitter (if one is lucky enough to find that commodity in the urban slop-houses of the multiple brewery chains) or to Guinness. They may, indeed, lack the strength and potency of the best Munich brews. But they are fine in a foaming flagon on a hot day, mostly of lager type, and the locals treat them with respect and discernment. Above all they go excellently with the great dishes of choucroute or a tangy potée. And certainly they breed bonhomie in the drinking-houses and *winstube*.

ACCOMMODATION

It is worth remembering that the French hotel industry is strictly controlled by the authorities: all hotels are inspected, registered, assessed, awarded their status in the hierarchy of luxury, and their prices are established. However dingy they may appear, they will be clean and, generally, reliable. They do not all have a restaurant, but all will provide a continental breakfast. Service charges and any taxes will automatically be included in the bill.

In most towns and cities there will be a cluster of hotels, covering almost the whole gamut of prices and luxury, around the station. In our region we found only one place where this was not so; in Mulhouse only very expensive hotels are to be found near the station, and cheaper ones, and there are but few of those, are tucked away in side streets, like poor relations, nearer the centre of the town.

Hotel-keepers will raise no objection to your seeing the room offered before you accept it. If they do object, there can be only one reason! My wife and I did, on one occasion, turn down a room, and my explanation, that we did not think it worth the price, left the manageress speechless with indignation.

Below we give a list of hotels in convenient centres. These we have either tried ourselves or looked at and considered agreeable. We have omitted the very expensive, the Frantels and the Mapotels, whose prices are only for the very rich, and the very rich will have no use for our humble advice. In the list hotels marked * * * will probably be in the 80-120 francs per night range, those marked * * will be roughly between 50-80 francs, and the * establishments may range between 35-50 francs, unless something dreadful happens to the rate of inflation in France, as well it may.

In alphabetical order of centres, then, here is the list.

COLMAR (our own favourite centre):

Park-Hotel, av. de la République ***, luxurious and modern.

Hotel Turenne, 10 rue de Bâle **, fairly modern and quite reasonable.

La Chaumière, 74 av. de la République, near the station, modest, with rooms arranged round a central courtyard. For its class very good toilet arrangements.

GÉRARDMER (not in the season!)

Hotel Viry, place des Déportés **, undistinguished but conveniently placed.

MULHOUSE

Hotel Wir, 1 porte de Bâle **, looks quite pleasant in an old-fashioned way, fairly central.

NANCY (the best centre for touring Lorraine)

Univers, 4 rue Carmes **, centrally placed, convenient and comfortable.

Central, close to the station *, usual bourgeois standards, dull décor; don't expect too much – the Frantel is just across the street.

RIBEAUVILLÉ (near – up in the mountains on the Ste-Marie-aux-Mines road)

La Pépinière **, rather expensive for its rating, but beautifully sited.

SAVERNE (quiet, but a pleasant centre for the northern hills)

Au Boeuf Noir, 22 Grand-rue **, well equipped and reasonably priced.

Hôtel de la Marne, 5 rue du Griffon *, aspidistras and brown varnish, but comfortable beds and spacious rooms for the price.

STRASBOURG (armies of hotels, the station square and approach streets are swarming with them, at all prices, some absurdly low, many elderly and probably struggling)

Monopole-Metropole, 16 rue Kuhn *** luxurious and a bit too pricey, but pleasant regional décor.

Vendôme, 9 place de la Gare **, one of the more modern near the station, but often full of tour parties.

(There are so many others all over the city that it is impossible to list even a representative selection).

VERDUN (an essential stopping place if you want to visit the battlefields)

Hostellèrie du Coq Hardi, av. de la Victoire **, comfortable, well turned out, recommended, not too pricey.

Poste et Pergola, av. Douaumont *, unpretentious but reasonable and well placed near the river.

Finally, for those who do their travelling by caravan, we mention again here the sites that we personally have used and liked.

Nancy: *Camping de Brabois*, 6 km s.w. on the Neufchâteau road (N.74). This is a fine, modern site set among trees. Excellent showers and loos, but arranged so much on the open plan that they are very draughty in cold weather.

Strasbourg: *Camping Montagne-Verte*, Rue Robert-Forrer, very close to the city and perhaps rather too close to the railway line. Good showers and loos (not draughty). Quite small and apt to be crowded.

Strasbourg: *Camping Baggersee*, off the N.68 towards Colmar, good, spacious, well appointed, on the lake side. Again apt to be crowded.

Apart from these that we can recommend, there are others well spoken of at Colmar, Gérardmer, Obernai, Phalsbourg and Ribeauvillé. However, if you follow our advice you will avoid the sites at Fraize and Corcieux.

But this is a region to explore, not just read about. So do go there. You will be delighted.

Et bonne chance à tous!

Bibliography

L'Alsace by Henri Nonn.
Découvrir la France series (Larousse) (Written in French).
Guide des Auberges et Logis de France (current edition).
Guide Gault-Millau (current edition).
Les Vosges et La Lorraine by Henri Nonn.
Michelin 'Green' Guide: Vosges, Alsace-Lorraine.
Michelin 'Red' Guide (current edition).
The Price of Glory by Alistair Horne (Penguin Edition 1978).

Index